MIRACLE
In My
LIVING ROOM

The Story of a Little Mann

EVELYN MANN

Miracle In My Living Room

Her Purpose Press
Publisher

is a part of the NOW Press Agency, Inc.
All inquiries can be made at www.nowpressagency.com

Printed in the United States of America.

ISBN: 978-0-9983944-0-4
E-BOOK ISBN: 978-0-9983944-1-1

First Edition

All the facts of this memoir are as I remember them. My storytelling is greatly enhanced by my husband's copious notes. The dialogue is not exact but to the best of my remembrance. The names of the doctors, nurses and the medical facilities have been changed for privacy.

Dedicated to my amazing husband, who is the unsung
hero of this story. His love for our son, can-do attitude,
and on-duty nights helps our son thrive.

Contents

Foreword to *Miracle in My Living Room*

I first met Evelyn seventeen years ago, and she was a very friendly and joyful Christian. After Ralph came into the picture, it wasn't long before I had the honor of marrying them. The following year, Evelyn became pregnant but then found out that her child was not "normal." I remember talking to Evelyn and Ralph and what struck me and encouraged me was their faith in the Lord. There was no way they would ever think of aborting their little baby—they were confident God was in charge and He was going to work everything out for good.

When Samuel was born, those early days were extremely challenging. But with friends at their side, a church in full support, a great medical team, and faith-filled prayers going up to the throne, God came through time and time again. Ralph and Evelyn knew that God was keeping little Samuel going and was helping them to be the parents they needed to be for this special child.

I will testify Ralph and Evelyn are incredible parents—from the delivery room to the NICU to their home. Rarely have I seen such faithful and dedicated parents. There have been so many trials, difficulties, and seemingly impossible situations. And always, Evelyn is there with Samuel and for Samuel. But what has moved her and energized her to keep taking care of her little boy? She knows Samuel is not just her boy but a wonderful gift from God. And she has a deep love for Samuel. Yes, a mother's love, but also a supernatural, God-given love for this miraculous child.

Evelyn's faithfulness, drive, perseverance, and continued caring has so amazed me. Now some will say, "Well, Samuel was not normal." But this is Evelyn's child and a child from God. He is normal to her, and by golly and by God's grace, she is going to take care of him. And she has. Is Evelyn perfect? Has she never worried? You know the answers. She has had fears, emotions, and bad days, but she has faith in a great God. She shows this faith by her prayers, by her perseverance, by her encouraging words, and by a God-positive attitude, which I have personally seen so many times.

Why does Evelyn have all this faith, love, joy, and perseverance? Because she has an incredible husband. Because she has continued support from her church. Because people are praying. But most importantly, because she knows her God, a good, faithful, powerful, and sovereign God, who has been with her all the way. She knows that God has been behind the scenes, working, strengthening, protecting, and helping her be the mother she needs to be. And Evelyn will say amen to this, that it is God who came through, God who blessed, and God who gets all the glory.

In these days, when there is less and less respect for life, when the weak, the needy, the disabled are too often neglected and disregarded, we need to be reminded all lives are special. God has a special purpose and plan for each life, for each child. And it is our God-given duty to take care of them, to raise them up by the grace of God and for the glory of God. God truly cares for all children, and might we be the instruments God uses to care for the ones He gives us.

I hope reading this book, *Miracle in Our Living Room*, will be a blessing to your life. I hope it will encourage you to trust God and to be faithful to the children God puts in your life. And as you are faithful, you too will see the grace of God, the blessings of God, and the glory of God.

Pastor Steve Hogan
Hope Bible Church of Tampa

Acknowledgments

The writing process is one I often equate to being pregnant, except that process only lasts nine months. The work you hold in your hand is representative of four years working to tell this true story well. My heartfelt thanks for not only those who helped in the writing process but also those who uplifted me in navigating an unthinkable circumstance.

I thank God for keeping my sweet boy full of life, for I could not have kept him alive by my sheer will. If there was a button to press to fix everything, I would have pressed it when I first found out my son's negative diagnosis. Instead, God has held my heart and my hand, giving me precious peace and proving, through my son's life, that miracles still happen.

Thanks to my husband for his dedication, love, and devotion not only for me but for our beautiful five-pound wonder, who changed our world. His ingenuity has earned him the title of Dad Guyver, which he has used in countless ways to make our son's life better. I'm grateful too for access to my husband's diary, from which I gleaned the fine details of this memoir.

Thank you to Now Press Agency for their heart and passion to bring my son's miracle into the hands of many. God sent you to me in His perfect timing knowing this story of inspiration should be told to bring hope to many families facing a similar circumstance. I appreciate your dedication to the story.

Thanks to the members of my Word Weavers group for faithfully offering feedback and encouragement. When I was ready to give up, your kind words uplifted me to write again. Special thanks to Janis Powell for her patience and time sharing with me about the art and craft of writing.

Thank you to my pastor and our church for cheering us on from the sidelines. The many times we received prayer for Samuel are too numerous to count. The meals provided in the hospital and after we brought Samuel home were welcomed and appreciated. The love showered on us and Samuel blessed us beyond measure. Special thanks to Charlotte Young, whose wise advice and listening ear were of great value to us.

Thank you to the Make-A-Wish Foundation, Lisa Andrews, Maria Mendivill, and Joe Pearl. Your heart for Samuel touches me still today. Your selfless act of volunteering your time and talents to create a memorable wish has helped us in ways you couldn't have known at the time. I will never forget what you did for our tiny family. Thanks to Lisa Andrews for continuing to include us in the Make-A-Wish family.

I would like to pay my gratitude to the medical community for all their dedication and devotion to my son. Including the doctors, nurses, and supporting staff at St. Joseph's Hospital NICU/PICU. With special thanks to Dr. Cartaya, Dr. Solomon, Dr. Kriseman, Dr. Riggs, Dr. Sheridan, and Dr. Cressman. You will forever hold a special place in my heart for advocating and believing in our little guy. Thank you to Dr. Hershberger for coming alongside me to bring Samuel into the world.

As I reflect on our journey, I'm extremely grateful for the amazing support of my former company, Progressive Insurance. From my supervisors, Kerry Chalk and Nick Di Pasquale, to all my co-workers, many of whom donated vacation hours for me to stay by Samuel's side, heartfelt thanks. The insurance coverage received from my self-insured company met all my son's medical needs, which I am forever grateful.

I would like to pay regards to Hector of Medicor—not only because he provided my son with all his home health equipment, but also because his unwavering belief in our son encouraged me. Hector was the first one to expect Samuel would come off his ventilator even before I believed it possible. And he did, but that is a story for another book. I continue to appreciate their care and concern for Samuel.

Anne Belloni, thank you for your faith in believing in our son even before he was born. You showed me what faith and praying believing looks like in real life. In the face of negative reports, your steadfastness buoyed my hope helping me to believe for the impossible.

Special thanks to those closest to our little guy. Our family and friends have seen our mini miracle defy the odds at every turn. Always ready with a listening ear, open arms, and many prayers, we have been truly blessed. Special thanks to my parents, Captain Ralf and Lucy Kraemer.

And finally, I would like to thank you, the reader, for taking the time to learn how a baby with a lethal form of dwarfism came to be a miracle. My desire is for my son's journey to not only inspire you but also encourage and give hope to others through these pages.

Chapter 1

THE TEST NO ONE WANTS TO TAKE!

"*Y*our child will die!" the doctor declared in the tiny pod of the neonatal intensive care unit. My mouth dropped open as my hands clenched by my side. I know I should respond, but I said nothing.

This battle between the doctor's predictions and my belief in the impossible is not new. The first hint of our child's challenges came early at my first ultrasound. I remember entering the Greenside Medical Services full of hope.

The waiting room had a few people in it.

"Do you think it's a boy or a girl?" I rushed on without waiting for my husband, Ralph, to answer. "I want a girl. We can name her Tina Maria Mann. Don't you think it has a nice ring to it?"

"I'm happy either way." He smiled.

A nurse called my name. She escorted me to an exam room to change into a standard-issue patient gown. I quickly donned the blue gown, excited to see my child for the first time. Exiting the changing room, the nurse motioned me into the sonogram room, where Ralph sat in a chair. He reached for my hand and squeezed it. I smiled.

Ralph helped me up on the table, and I laid back. The technician put the cold gel on my skin and spread it around. When she placed the probe on my ever-expanding belly, an image appeared on the screen. We strained to make it out.

We had never seen a pregnancy sonogram before. We didn't know what to look for. Where was the head? Was the baby a boy or a girl? We couldn't tell from the blur of black-and-white images. The technician remained silent.

After a few minutes, she made sounds we couldn't understand. Spanish, maybe? I thought she would tell us our child's gender, but she didn't utter a word. Perhaps she wanted the doctor to share the news.

After several moments of silence, she motioned for me to get dressed. Back in my street clothes, I found Ralph in the doctor's office instead of the reception area. We waited for what seemed like hours, but it might have been as short as twenty minutes. I should have realized something was wrong.

The doctor came in with a computer printout in his hand. My first impression of the doctor did not elicit confidence. His medium build and mass of wild hair looked like he had been trying to pull it out on each side.

He repositioned his glasses and said, "The good news, Mrs. Mann, is you are going to have a boy."

I looked over at Ralph, who couldn't hide his grin.

"However, your child is not developing normally."

I held my breath, balancing on the edge of my chair. Why was the doctor only speaking directly to me? Ralph was not a small man. His large six-foot-tall frame could be perceived as intimidating if it weren't for his kind smile and warm laugh. He was neither smiling nor laughing at this point.

"His arms and legs are thirty percent behind where they should be at week twenty."

I gripped the arms of my chair. "Can't they catch up?"

"Yes, however, he's so far behind at this point it's unlikely he will."

My brain scrambled to understand the ramifications. All we came to find out was whether we were having a boy or a girl.

I tried to focus on the doctor again. "Also, there may be another problem because his head is not perfectly round. I recommend you have a high-level sonogram performed to assess your child further. We can do it here, but you must make a new appointment. Do you have any other questions for me?"

I stammered. "No, thank you for meeting with us." All I wanted was to escape and never see him again.

We made no follow-up appointment.

How could this be? A problem with our first precious child? A boy.

By the time we drove away, the pressure in my chest made me feel like I wanted to explode. "Can you believe the doctor? He didn't even look at you."

"I noticed that too. Maybe we should get a second opinion."

"Yes, but I'm never going back there!"

We had no idea how our faith would be tested.

Chapter 2

THROUGH EVERYTHING; A NEW CREATION

*A*s much as I didn't want to believe the doctor's news about our son, concern controlled my thoughts. Being pregnant only heightened my emotions. As I drove home after work, a thought came to mind.

Maybe I should drive off the road and hit a tree. That would take care of everything.

My breath shallowed, and I blinked. How could I even think about doing something so drastic? I tried to focus on the road. *I have to tell Ralph. But what would he think of me? Would he think I'm crazy?*

After pulling in the drive, I rested my forehead on the steering wheel. *I must overcome my fear and tell Ralph.*

Finding Ralph sitting on the couch, I took his hands in mine and told him what happened. I stared at his hands while I shared my embarrassing moment. When I looked up, not only did he not turn away from me, but he confessed to having his own internal struggle.

Holding my face in his hands, he kissed my forehead. "We're going to be okay. We'll handle this together."

Relief swept over me, and I hugged him tight. "I know, you're right. I'm so glad you're here for me."

After we talked, the negative thoughts never returned.

Facing questions about my pregnancy made me cringe. How did I answer when asked "How are you doing?" or "How is the baby doing?" I tried to answer these questions positively, but inside, I wasn't so sure.

One coworker who did not know about my circumstances mentioned a TV special on odd medical problems that can occur during pregnancy. I wanted to run in other direction, but my feet wouldn't move. Should I tell her to stop? Should I explain the bad news about my son's growth? Not able to hold back any longer, I told my coworker I had to get back to work. At my desk, I closed my eyes and let out a sigh. I vowed to never do that to another pregnant woman.

Soon the day came for our appointment at Orlando Healthcare Diagnostics.

A nurse escorted me to the sonogram room, where Ralph joined me, as well as three nurses and a doctor. Their faces showed no joy. At one point during the sonogram, our son waved at us. There also was no question our baby was a boy. The sonogram technician stated, "He is very proud of himself!"

After a thorough exam, the doctor looked at me and said, "I wish I had better news for you, but it appears your son has a lethal form of dwarfism. We don't know what kind, but it does not seem to be compatible with life. I am so sorry, Mrs. Mann." He hung his head as he left the room. The nurses scurried about, and one said I could change to meet with the genetic counselor.

I heard the doctor's words, but my heart did not accept their implication. I oddly felt incubated and at peace in the middle of the storm. One nurse said she too sensed peace in the room as if a calming angel had arrived.

After getting dressed, we met with James Blake, the genetic counselor. His office had a simple desk against the wall by the door.

We each sat in a chair by the window. Light streamed into the small space. I longed to be in the sunlight, feeling the warmth of the sun going into my bones. My attention was drawn back to Dr. Blake, who was looking at my chart. He asked us a series of questions about our health history and drew a chart of our family histories.

"Well," Dr. Blake concluded, "it does not look like your family history has any bearing on your son having dwarfism. Looking at his sonogram, we can only guess at what form of dwarfism is involved here. The sonogram results show your son's body is three weeks advanced in growth, but his limbs are three weeks behind. The kidney looks pinched. My best guess is your son may have Osteogenesis Imperfecta, Jeune Syndrome, or Thanatophoric Dwarfism." He described each potential diagnosis. "Osteogenesis Imperfecta (OI) is known as brittle bone disease and is a genetic bone disorder. These children's bones break very easy. OI is survivable. Jeune syndrome is a condition where the thoracic is blocked off and the child dies from asphyxiation at birth. The third is Thanatophoric Dysplasia, where the child's lungs are severely compromised, with most children not surviving birth." As he rattled off these diagnoses, my mind reeled, trying to follow along.

"Your son could have a potentially lethal skeletal dysplasia."

Later we received the report of our meeting, which also stated our son could have Triploidy, where a fetus has sixty-nine chromosomes instead of forty-six. This condition is also "not compatible with life."

"Would you consider a therapeutic abortion?" he said. I had never heard of a therapeutic abortion before. I had to look it up after the appointment.

"No, we will not consider an abortion," I said. "We will have this baby no matter what the outcome is," I continued as my husband nodded in agreement.

Dr. Blake went on to tell us we should get an amniocentesis. Since reports show one in two hundred amniocenteses result in harm to the baby, we agreed to not risk it. We determined to go ahead with the pregnancy and did not feel any test result would change our mind.

Then he asked me a surprising question, "Do you have faith?"

I choked up, embarrassed as tears fell down my cheeks. To this point, no medical professional had asked me this question.

"Yes, we have faith in God," I said as the words tumbled out of me. "I believe everything is going to work out," I stated with conviction. My husband nodded in agreement.

"Well, that's good. Hang on to your faith," he said with a smile. "Now, how do we pinpoint what kind of dwarfism we have here? We recommend an x-ray called a fetogram, which determines bone strength. Once this report is completed, it needs to be read by an experienced doctor who knows what to look for on the scan. If we do not have an expert read the report, it will all be for nothing," he stressed. "Dr. Jack Aaron is an expert in evaluating and diagnosing skeletal dysplasias. He is your best bet to read the report correctly. The fetogram should be done by twenty-six to twenty-eight weeks to improve the chances of obtaining adequate views."

After finishing with the doctor and heading outside, we looked at each other and hugged. The most incredible feeling of peace overwhelmed me. I just knew deep down inside everything would be okay. No medical evidence supported my confidence.

And the peace of God, which transcends all understanding, will guard your hearts and your minds in Christ Jesus Philippians 4:7, NIV.

In the moment after hearing such discouraging news about our son, I experienced this supernatural peace that transcended all understanding. This peace didn't make sense, given the circumstances. I had never experienced a peace like this before and would not soon forget it.

We left the doctor's office and went to a restaurant for a late lunch. As we waited for the food to arrive, I told Ralph about the amazing sense of peace I experienced.

"That's funny," he said, surprised, "because I felt the same thing."

"Really?"

"Yes." he replied, smiling.

The peace I experienced would carry me through many days to come.

—⟨∿⟩—

As my pregnancy progressed, I visited my gynecologist more often. At one appointment, Dr. Michaels encouraged us to meet with the neonatologist at the local hospital.

On a spring Florida day, we met Dr. Davidson at Riverside Metropolitan Hospital.

As he greeted us, I instantly liked his warm smile and firm handshake.

He sat down in a reclining office chair. "So how can I help you?"

We sat in two empty chairs opposite the doctor. Ralph and I looked at each other, not knowing how to answer. My doctor didn't explain the purpose of this meeting.

I stammered, "Well, we are not sure how you can help us. We had a high-level sonogram in Orlando and were told our son may have a lethal form of skeletal dysplasia."

After sharing the report from our genetic counselor, the doctor gave us his recommendations.

"We could treat your son here, but we don't have an ECMO [extracorporeal membrane oxygenation] machine. If your son requires extra oxygen for his heart and lungs to function properly, this machine takes out the blood, oxygenates it, and returns it to the body."

I took a deep breath. Ralph leaned forward in his chair. His face turned pale.

"If you want an ECMO machine available, you will need to deliver at either Gulfside Hospital or Lakefront Children's Hospital in St. Petersburg."

He paused to gauge our reaction. We didn't ask any questions.

He continued, "If you choose to deliver here, understand I will work with what I am dealt. Sometimes parents ask for extreme measures when I know they won't work."

We'll take our chances.

Dr. Davidson leaned back in his chair. "Do you want to go to a hospital with an ECMO machine or deliver here?"

"I don't want to put our son through this procedure," Ralph said firmly, a little color returning to his face. "We will deliver here."

"Do you want us to use all measures to keep your son alive?"

We both nodded in agreement. "Absolutely."

"Well, then, that is what we will do," he said. He stood up, ending the meeting.

By week twenty, our son wasn't growing. The news from doctors caused us to rely on our faith. We heard of a local church conference coming to Tampa. Trying to find hope where I could, I thought, why not go?

Before entering the sanctuary one night, I spoke to one of the volunteers at the book table. I told her the predictions our son would not live. She listened politely and told me she would pray. The next night, I saw this dear lady in the lobby. She told me she had something to give me. From behind the book counter, she produced a pair of baby-blue hand mittens. She handed them to me, telling me the Lord told her our son would use these mittens. I gave her a hug and thanked her for the gift. Her statement of faith gave me much-needed hope.

Returning for another sonogram, I lay on the exam table with the room dark except the glare from the black-and-white images on the screen. Ralph leaned closer to the screen. Reid, the sonographer, looked up at the screen and explained the images. Her Southern drawl soothed me. After taking several measurements, I asked, "Has he grown any?"

"No, the measurements are the same." My heart sunk.

"I can see he is breathing very well." My heart sang.

"His chest cavity is still smaller than it should be. His head is a little big, but nothing I'd be concerned about right now."

Bad news. Good news. Bad news. Good news. My emotions pulled in two different directions.

Reid pulled a strand of curly hair behind her ear and typed on the sonogram keyboard. "The reason you are measuring five weeks ahead of schedule is because you have excess amniotic fluid in your belly. Dr. Kelly will tell you more about it." What did excess fluid have to do with the progression of my pregnancy?

After getting dressed, we sat in the waiting room. Dr. Kelly, a petite woman with blond hair wearing a white overcoat, greeted us. She led us to an exam room. After looking at my thick medical record, the questioning began.

"Have you decided on a delivery plan yet?" the doctor asked.

"No," Ralph answered for me.

"Am I treating one patient or two?"

My mind whirled. What did she mean? Was she trying to save me only or both me and my son? Could she actually think we did not want to save our son?

"I need to know," the doctor said, speaking directly to Ralph, "in case I have to filet your wife open. Do you really want me to perform an emergency C-section just to have the baby die five minutes later?"

"I do not want my wife fileted open," Ralph said firmly.

"You know having such a serious surgery could affect future pregnancies," she countered. "When can you give me an answer on what you want me to do? By next week?"

"We will let you know when we are ready." Thankfully, Ralph answered all her questions. Her tone kept me silent. Ralph protected me.

I tuned out the rest of the meeting. My only objective was to leave. A burning sensation filled my chest, but it was not indigestion. Ralph offered to drive home.

Once in the car, I burst out, "I think she believes the baby is going to die. I am not sure I want her delivering our child."

"I think you're right, but I can see why she believes the baby is not going to make it based on the possible diagnosis."

I silently agreed with Ralph's assessment begrudgingly.

Ralph continued, "I agree we need a more optimistic person delivering our child."

That's an understatement!

I threw my hands in the air. "How we can be sure she won't be the one to deliver? Whoever is on call at birth will deliver. I want a doctor who believes our child will live."

"We won't know. We'll have to wait and see what happens. In the meantime, we pray."

I shifted in my seat. I knew Ralph was right.

Ralph placed his hand on my knee. "I was encouraged by Reid's words. Did you hear her say, 'The movie is not over yet?' She also said 'There is a life in there.'"

Dr. Kelly's words dominated my thoughts. I forgot about the encouragement Reid gave us.

"You're right. She was amazing. I agree with her. Now if only the doctors could catch her vision."

For a moment, hope filled my heart, temporarily blocking out Dr. Kelly's harsh words.

Hearing all the reports regarding our son's diagnosis caused us to draw on our faith. We both came to faith at different times in our lives. Ralph was raised in Detroit, Michigan. One night when he was a teenager, sitting in a tree swing, Ralph said, "God, if you are real, I will believe in you." Soon after moving to Tampa, his family attended a local church, where a gospel presentation confirmed his commitment to Jesus Christ. New in the faith, his family traveled to Jerusalem for a memorable journey. Seeing the pages of the Bible come alive during the trip made an impact on him for life.

When I was nine years old, I encountered a stranger. I lived on a forty-one-foot sailboat, and on this particular weekend, we were anchored off an island near the western coast of Canada. The stranger was from a boat filled with a group of missionaries. He walked to me as I played on the dock.

"Hi, my name is Ron. What is your name?"

"Evelyn."

"Nice to meet you, Evelyn. Can I ask you a question?"

"Sure."

"Do you know who Jesus Christ is?"

"No."

"He is a wonderful man who lived a long time ago. He walked on water and did many miracles. He has a wonderful plan for your life. Would you like to learn more about Jesus?"

"Sure."

"How about I send you a book about him?"

As a young nine-year-old girl, my father instilled in me a love for reading, so when Ron mentioned a book, he had my attention.

"That would be great!"

"If you give me your address, I will send you the book. How does that sound?"

"Super!"

Even at my age, I was skeptical Ron would fulfill his promise. To my amazement, two weeks later, I received a book in the mail. The cover had a picture of Jesus carrying a lamb on it. My father said I took to reading the Bible like a duck takes to water. Though I loved it, I oftentimes did not understand its meaning. I read about the Ten Commandments but had difficulty living by them. As I grew older, I felt trapped in a cycle of sin, resulting in repeated apologies to God, which left me wanting.

Twenty years after receiving the book, I was alone in my apartment one day. I reached a point where I saw my life as a piece of broken glass shattered beyond repair. It was then I told God he could have all of me. I asked him to repair the broken glass of my life. Afterward, I felt at peace. Even if I awoke at three in the morning, I knew I was not alone. I had become a new creation in Christ.

Chapter 3

WARNING: OBJECTS MAY APPEAR LARGER THAN THEY ARE

*I*n between doctors' appointments, life continued. We attended a weekend church conference, took the car in for repairs, and went shopping for clothes to accommodate my growing belly. Being four months pregnant, I was showing; however, most of the maternity clothes looked like they were fitted for someone much further along. The store had a solution for such a dilemma: the clerk gave me a padded pillow made to strap around my belly.

Excited to see what I would look like, I put the fake baby belly on and slid into a flowing dress. Looking in the mirror, I laughed. Surely this would be not what I would look like fully pregnant. The image staring back at me reflected my full five-foot-two frame engulfed in a mass of floral print, losing any semblance of my figure. I placed my hands under the fake belly to see what I might look like in the near future. The image looked out of proportion for my body. *Oh, well*, I thought, *it was worth a try*. When I asked the saleslady about the fake belly, she said they give the customer an idea of what they might look like. For that moment, I enjoyed being a pregnant lady maternity shopping. I didn't think about doctors' appointments, a negative diagnosis, or potential outcomes. Instead, I chuckled as I left the store thinking of my image in the mirror. They should have a disclaimer put on the mirror in the dressing room stating "Warning: Objects may appear larger than they are."

The month of June brought yet another doctor's appointment. Holding my breath, I tried to brace myself for another battle. My previous visit with Dr. Kelly still made me want to run.

I signed in. Shortly after, a nurse took me back to her office, and she opened my rather thick file. The folder was stamped High Risk in large red letters.

After some informal questions, she asked, "Mrs. Mann, from our records, I see you have not written a life support plan."

I didn't realize I was being asked whether I wanted palliative care or medical intervention for my son at birth. "No, I haven't, and I don't want to," I replied firmly. She continued to look at my file shaking her head, showing her disapproval.

Soon after, Ellen, who introduced herself as the midwife, escorted me to an exam room. I explained the pressure I felt to make a life support plan.

"You will be asked again," Ellen replied to my complaint. "However, when they ask, you can say you are not prepared to make this decision now."

"I didn't know if I *had* to give them an answer," I said, making a mental note for my next meeting. "I don't really know what is going to happen when our son is born, but we really believe he is going to live. I know it looks impossible to the doctors, but I know that nothing is impossible with God." I paused. How would Ellen respond? We'd never met before, but I couldn't hold back the words. She looked sweet enough. Cropped blond hair framed her face, and her eyes had a kindness to them. I didn't have to wait long for my answer.

"I believe in the power of prayer. I have seen prayer answered many times."

I didn't expect Ellen to agree. Many times when I commented

about my faith, I received no reaction. And here was Ellen, while not saying my son would live, she validated my faith.

She continued, "You could even have someone praying while the baby is being delivered. I know the number of people in the delivery room is limited, but you can probably have one more person there too."

I leaned forward in my chair. "I never considered having someone praying for me in the delivery room." Thankful I had someone who seemed to understand, I bared more of my soul to this dear person. "Every time I come to visit the doctor, I am hearing something negative about my son. No one seems to have hope except my husband and I. Recently a good friend told me about her pregnancy. There was a concern her unborn baby was at risk for infection. Her doctor said it was his job to worry about the pregnancy, not hers. I wish I could say the same. I try not to stress out, but I do every time I come here."

She nodded. "I believe the medical community doesn't take childbirth as a natural part of a woman's life. They are clinical in their approach to pregnancy, almost to the point of being inhuman. You are fortunate to be pregnant."

Perhaps she was speaking to my advanced maternal age of thirty-nine.

"This is your pregnancy. Enjoy it."

Touched by her encouragement, wetness trickled down my cheeks. "Sorry about the tears." I wiped the embarrassing tears away with the palm of my hand.

Ellen gave me a Kleenex. "No, it is okay. You are pregnant. It is natural to cry." Her motherly tone comforted me.

We hugged, and I went to the checkout desk. The receptionist took the yellow sheet of paper documenting today's visit. She looked at the paper and then at my chart.

"Was your file stamped High Risk today?" she asked.

"No, I don't think so."

She mumbled, but I'm sure I heard her say, "You weren't supposed to see her."

I guess midwives don't handle high-risk cases. This "mistake" brought me hope. Meeting Ellen was something God allowed to happen because he knew my desperate need for encouragement.

Being a first-time mother, I wanted to experience a natural childbirth. But how safe is natural childbirth versus a Cesarean section? As with any big decision, we wanted another opinion, a second opinion. Being well past thirty weeks of gestation, I began to search for another doctor to advise us. I called several places, only to be told they would not take new cases after thirty weeks or they would not take high-risk cases at all.

A friend gave me the name of a prolife doctor. I called the office and explained my situation to the nurse. I simply wanted a second opinion. Would the doctor meet with us? She said she would consult with him and get back to me.

A few days later, she called back.

"Mrs. Mann, I talked to the doctor about your case. He would like to help you, but his hands are tied. He consulted with his lawyer, who advised against it."

I wasn't sure I heard her correctly.

"If my husband and I sign a waiver, would that work?"

"Well, actually, no. The lawyer said if we advise you in this case and something goes wrong, once the baby becomes eighteen years old, he could sue."

How could our son sign a waiver since he was still in my belly? Even though I knew this is impossible, the thought popped

Several years later, I understood why the doctor would not see me. In 2011, a 25-year-old Australian woman sued her mother's doctor for not delivering her via C-section. She was delivered with forceps which caused an injury leaving her without full use of her arm. In 2005, I just could not foresee such a lawsuit being a possibility.

into my mind. It's odd what you think about when faced with an unthinkable circumstance. With no other option available, I replied, "Okay, thank you for trying."

"We really wanted to help you. We wish you all the best."

Her words offered me no comfort.

Thirty weeks into my pregnancy, my belly swelled like a balloon and was expanding at a faster rate than was considered safe. My doctor explained polyhydramnios is an excess of amniotic fluid in the amniotic sac. My son was not breathing the fluid properly due to his limited chest size. His small chest size was not able to hold all his organs, causing the trachea and the esophagus to be crowded. This condition could lead to premature labor as well as an increase in perinatal mortality. *Lovely, more bad news,* I thought.

Several doctors discussed how to alleviate the excess of amniotic fluid. One choice was to do nothing. Another choice was to perform a therapeutic amniocentesis. This procedure would draw out excess amniotic fluid. Remove the excess fluid, resolve the problem. One doctor advised us to not perform this procedure because the relief experienced is short-term. The fluid could come back in as soon as two days, bringing us back to square one. After much discussion, the doctors prescribed strict bed rest for a week with a follow-up appointment to measure growth.

At home, I followed the doctor's orders. Lying on the couch with a view of my expanding belly and the back porch, I wondered if this pregnancy would ever end. My dear husband tackled the cooking and cleaning and kept me happy. He never complained. I have a little secret: my husband is the real unsung hero. God couldn't have picked a better husband and soon-to-be father, the proof being clearly seen with each passing day.

Chapter 4

SAMUEL WILL USE THIS

O
ne night, I noticed something different.
Shaking Ralph awake, I said, "Honey, I think I am leaking fluid."
He rubbed his eyes, straining to wake up.

I continued, "I don't think my water broke. What should I do?"

"Why don't you call the doctor tomorrow? Have the baby checked out to put your mind at ease."

I rubbed my eyes. "I can't do anything about it right now. I'll call first thing."

Somehow, I fell back asleep. Waking to the sun streaming into the bedroom, I jolted awake. The clock read 7:30a.m. Too soon to call the doctor. "I guess I will have breakfast first," I mumbled, realizing Ralph already left for work.

Entering the kitchen, I poured a small glass of orange juice. *If only I could enjoy a cup of tea. It tastes so bitter to me now. Could it be the pregnancy?* I heard of pregnant women having food cravings, but I never heard anyone having an aversion to tea.

After breakfast, I leaned back on the couch and waited for the doctor's office to open. I laid my hand on my belly. What would the doctor say this time? I didn't know if I could handle another bad report. A verse came to mind: "Cast your burden upon the Lord and He shall sustain thee." I closed my eyes. "Yes, Lord, you will sustain me." A calm settled over me, banishing away my anxiety. I looked up at the clock. 9:00a.m. Time to call the doctor. It was July 7, 2005. The nurse scheduled me for their first available appointment.

We arrived for our 11:45a.m. appointment. Dr. Nicholson conducted an exam, taking a test sample.

"I suspect you are leaking amniotic fluid. We will wait for test results. In the meantime, the nurse is going to monitor the baby and see how he is doing, okay?"

Dr. Nicholson's tone put me at ease. Roughly the same age as my husband, his genuine smile and kind bedside manner made me feel better.

"Okay."

The doctor gently touched my shoulder and left the room. The nurse placed a wide elastic belt on my round belly. A machine next to me registered a needle moving up and down while my husband and I looked on. I wasn't sure what the needle going up and down meant. Was up good and down bad? After ten minutes, the nurse came in and read the ticker tape. "Mrs. Mann, the baby does not seem to be in distress. We are just waiting on your test results. The doctor will be in a few minutes."

I looked at Ralph, relieved. Maybe we could go home soon. We talked quietly while waiting for the doctor.

Twenty minutes later, the doctor returned with my chart in his hand.

"At first, the results of your test came back negative. I decided to wait for the slide to dry and retest. The second test came back positive. You are leaking amniotic fluid."

Dr. Nicholson paused, gaging my response. I wondered what this could mean. The doctor continued, "The baby is not in distress, but we do recommend you check into the hospital for observation."

"This is surreal," I said to Ralph as he drove me to the hospital. "I am only in my thirty-first week."

"I know. I didn't expect the doctor to send you to the hospital."

Once we arrived at the hospital, I checked in and was asked to wait while a room was being prepared.

In the large open atrium, I noticed two other pregnant ladies. They appeared calm. No one rushed.

I changed and was taken to a room full of equipment with a hospital bed in the middle. I lay down, pulling the hospital gown close around my frame. The nurse strapped a belt on my belly to monitor the baby's heartbeat and to check for contractions. The monitor showed some contractions, but I could not feel them. Ralph joined me.

After a flurry of activity and a few tests to boot, the head nurse, Jacqueline, came to speak to us.

"In case your son is delivered, the doctor wants to give him medicine to help his lungs get the extra boost they need to develop. If it is all right with you both, I will administer it."

I looked at Ralph, who was nodding yes.

"Of course. We want to do anything to help our son," I said.

Another nurse, who checked my vitals, said, "With a high leak, the baby can be delivered in as soon as three days." I stored this information in my heart, praying this would not be true in my case.

Someone brought Ralph a cot so he could stay with me in the room. I needed him close to me. After several hours, we found out the contractions were due to dehydration, but they kept me in the delivery room all night. I dozed off several times; however, deep sleep eluded me because the nurses kept checking on me. By morning, Ralph turned his cot back in. Since it was determined Samuel would not make his appearance, I was transferred to a regular room on the fifth floor.

The next day a doctor visited me from the Diagnostic Consulting Group.

"Hello, Mrs. Mann, my name is Dr. Shimer. I have looked at your son's sonograms and have reviewed all the available documentation."

I reclined on the bed, a captive audience for the nice doctor. I welcomed another set of eyes to review our case.

"I am not sure your son has a fatal form of dwarfism." He paused briefly, allowing me to absorb the statement. "The shape of your son's head does not fall in the category of a fatal diagnosis, to my knowledge."

I was still silent; however, my heart swelled with hope. Finally, someone who agreed our son will not die at birth.

Dr. Shimer opened my door. Surprised to see him so soon after our meeting yesterday, I waved him in. He explained, after re-reviewing the data, perhaps he was wrong about his assessment. There was still a possibility my son had a fatal diagnosis. He exited the room leaving me stunned. The hope I felt yesterday deflated. Would not one medical professional agree our son would survive?

More than three days passed, and Samuel hadn't made his appearance. The staff daily monitored my son's progress. A nurse strapped a large belt around my belly with probes linked to a monitoring machine. It registered a graph with readings only a nurse could decipher. One day, the nurse could not detect movement from Samuel.

Even though I assured the nurse I was still pregnant, she scheduled the sonogram. My son swam in a sea of excess fluid his little lungs were not able to process. Perhaps this was why they could not find him. I did not experience the delight of feeling him move or kick his little feet in my belly. Just one more reminder this pregnancy was different.

At radiology, a technician asked me to recline on the table. I felt like a beached whale.

"Are you comfortable?" she asked.

"Not exactly."

"Well, this shouldn't take long."

She started moving her wand on my rotund abdomen.

"Can you shift to the right?"

I shifted.

"Now the left."

I obeyed.

"Can you move your stomach to the left and then to the right?"

I jiggled my belly.

"Ah, there he is."

Oh, good. Finally.

The technician, being satisfied with the result, sent me back to my room. The next day, the same routine occurred. On the third day, the technician turned on the 3-D switch and caught a sight of Samuel in a full pout. Maybe he did not like the roller coaster antics to get him moving. The technician, captivated, printed the image and shared it with her coworkers. She handed me a copy for the scrapbook.

By the third sonogram, I told the staff I had an idea: put the belt on my belly in the afternoon. My son was clearly not a morning person, much like his mother. The nurses relented. I was the only pregnant woman to be monitored in the afternoon. Sure enough, they were able to detect movement.

After much deliberation, we decided to deliver Samuel via C-section as the safest option. The next question became when to deliver, at thirty-two weeks or thirty-five weeks? The doctors' main concern centered around if I would develop an infection, which could harm Samuel and result in an emergency C-section. I didn't feel in control of the decision but relied on the experts to choose. When I heard of a potential delivery date at thirty-two weeks, I felt unsettled by the idea. How I *felt* didn't factor into the doctors' decision. Though not an expert, my momma instinct kicked in.

During this time, Ralph and I would often read the Bible and pray together. After all, Samuel's life rested in God's hands. We chose to place our trust in him despite all the negative reports.

After considerable discussion, the doctors set a delivery date of thirty-five weeks. My surgery date was scheduled for August 2, 2005.

We notified our family. Ralph shared the news with our pastor. A call to Linda, the prayer coordinator, activated the church prayer chain. I called my close friend Anne, who made arrangements to fly to Florida from Texas. She assured me she would pray during the delivery. I knew she couldn't be in the delivery room, but her support helped me breathe a bit easier.

The day before Samuel's birth, Anne bought an infant car seat and brought it to the hospital room. She predicted, "Samuel will use this!"

The Bible describes faith as "being sure of what we hope for and certain of what we do not see" (Hebrews 11:1, NIV). We could not see Samuel would make it past birth, but we believed. I cherished Anne coming alongside me to believe everything would be okay. In the face of Samuel's dire diagnosis, her faith bolstered my own.

Chapter 5

THE DAY WE WELCOMED SAMUEL INTO THE WORLD

I'm not an early riser; however, on this special day, my morning started before sunrise. Surgery was set for 7:00a.m. A nurse helped me get ready to go to pre-op as Ralph packed my belongings to be moved to another room. He wasn't allowed to be with me when I would get the epidural, although I would have appreciated him holding my hand. After the sedative pulsed through my body, I panicked at my loss of control. Tears streamed down my face. Susan, the nurse, held my hand and talked into my ear.

"You're doing fine. You're doing just great."

Her soothing tone and calm voice gave me peace as though an angel had spoken. The epidural's effect numbed me from my chest down like a heavy blanket. I was surprisingly warm, though the room temperature hovered at sixty degrees.

After I was wheeled into the operating room, Ralph arrived in scrubs. His smiling brown eyes peeked out from behind the mask covering his face. His presence comforted me. A sheet blocked the view of my belly.

Dr. Michaels and Dr. Johnson stood on either side of me. I should feel special having two doctors in attendance, but my mind was focused on what would happen next. Including the doctors, ten medical personnel were ready to bring Samuel into the world.

24

"Everyone ready to go?" Dr. Michaels said. He looked over the curtain. "Are you ready?"

I smiled and nodded yes. I was ready to hear Samuel cry out loud. For months I had been praying to hear Samuel's cry of life.

"You shouldn't feel anything, only some pressure."

I nodded again.

A tugging sensation rocked my body from side to side, but I didn't feel any pain. I heard a whoosh of my water breaking, gallons of excess fluid flooding the floor.

Samuel entered the world at 8:03a.m.

I listened for Samuel's cry but didn't hear it. I searched Ralph's face for answers.

"What's happening?"

He looks over the sheet.

"They're checking everything out."

Lord, please, Lord, help Samuel breathe.

Is my son breathing? Why didn't I hear him cry? I sensed movement next to me to find a nurse holding Samuel on my right side. His body was completely wrapped in a towel, and I couldn't see his arms or legs. His face was bright red, and his eyes were squeezed tight from crying. Before I could fully absorb his beauty, the nurse took him away to the neonatal intensive care unit.

Dr. Michaels touched my shoulder. "We're all done here. You did great. The nurses will finish up and take you to recovery."

Though I couldn't see his lips move behind the surgery mask, I could see a smile in his eyes.

"Thank you for everything." I wanted to say more, but no words came.

I was taken to a new room on the third floor. As I got settled in, a frantic question would not go away. *When will I see my son again?*

The staff, concerned about our son's tenuous grip on life, suggested I see Samuel as soon as possible. To protect my C-section incision, the nurse devised a plan to wheel me into the neonatal intensive care unit (NICU) in my hospital bed.

I didn't notice the other children in the seven-crib unit or their accompanying alarms, nurses, and staff. The nurse pushed my huge hospital bed next to a crib. My son's small form was tucked in a u-shaped blanket. His head, covered with black strands of hair, faced away from me.

Wires circled various ways. A tube entered his lips, held by a plastic mouthpiece taped to each cheek. It led to a ventilator delivering each breath to keep Samuel oxygenated and his lungs inflated. His foot had a brown fabric probe wrapped around it with a red light reading his oxygen level and heart rate.

A lead on his chest went to a monitor displaying his vitals on a screen above the crib. A heart-shaped patch on his chest measured his temperature. His sleeping form seemed undisturbed by all the wires and monitors surrounding him.

I reached over and touched his soft, smooth skin. Beautiful. I stared in awe at the miracle before me. I could spend all day looking at him.

A nurse took a picture of us, Ralph on one side of the crib, Samuel in the middle, and me in the hospital bed on the other side. Our first family portrait. Too soon, the nurse wheeled me back to my room.

When I woke, Ralph was sitting in a chair next to my hospital bed.

"How is Samuel doing?"

"He is holding his own. I got to change his diaper."

I smiled at the image of my six-foot-tall husband changing his five-pound son's diaper for the first time.

"The nurse took a picture. My first official act as a father."

I touched Ralph's arm. "We'll have to put it in Samuel's photo album."

On Samuel's second day of life, a nurse said I could hold him for the first time. He was still in critical condition, but I was somehow oblivious to it all. All I could think about was holding him close to my chest.

The nurse brought in a large purple rocking chair. Ralph stood behind me.

"Mom, if you sit here, I'll take care of everything. I'm going to secure Samuel's wires to the chair so they won't come loose."

After unhooking his connections, she gently lowered him into my arms.

I gazed into my precious son's face. Every few seconds, his facial expression changed, from wrinkling his nose to looking at me wide-eyed. Pure joy filled me. Was this what being a mother felt like?

Realizing how small and fragile he was, a twinge of fear went through me. I wasn't hurting him, was I? Samuel's monitor above me registered his heart rate, temperature, and oxygen level. As I glanced up at the screen, the monitor emitted a loud, piercing sound. I searched for his nurse, wanting to know what was wrong. She appeared in seconds.

"Everything is fine, Mom. We just need to put him back in the crib now."

So soon?

"Don't worry, you'll hold him again."

"I can't wait."

She placed him back in the crib, making several adjustments, silencing his alarms. Knowing he was all right, we went back to the hospital room.

Samuel's birth certificate waited for our signature. A simple act, a victorious moment.

Pastor Hogan was visiting during the evening shift, when Dr. Johnson entered my hospital room.

"Do you mind if I give you an update with your company here?"

Ralph responded, "Sure, no problem."

"There's a strong possibility your son will need continuous assisted breathing. This means he'll need a mobile device to breathe and may need to be institutionalized."

I sensed my heart beating in my ears.

Pastor Steve looked at the doctor with a blank stare.

"Do you have any questions?" the doctor asked.

Ralph replied, "No, Doctor, no questions."

I looked up. "I don't believe it."

Ralph touched my arm. "We'll wait and see."

I walked into the house after a month of living in the hospital. Everything looked the same except I was not pregnant anymore.

It was good to be home.

When Ralph retrieved the rented breast pump from the car, we cleaned and sterilized it. After reading the instructions, I attempted to follow the steps, without success. Knowing my breast milk was important for Samuel's development added to my frustration.

"Now what am I going to do?"

"Honey, don't be so hard on yourself. You're going through a lot right now. Just try again tomorrow."

He pulled me close, giving me a hug. I relaxed.

"I know you're right, my love."

My emotions tugged on my heart to go back to the hospital. I changed clothes, and we drove seven miles to see our son again.

Dr. Stone was in the NICU when we arrived.

I shook his hand. "Hi, Dr. Stone, thank you for all you are doing for Samuel."

"Any compliments should be directed to Him." He pointed to the ceiling. Ralph and I looked at each other, stunned.

"So true." Ralph nodded in agreement.

Did someone tell Dr. Stone about our faith? Another doctor perhaps?

His acknowledgment of faith encouraged me.

Chapter 6

D-DAY! (DIAGNOSIS DAY)

*A*larms rang as we entered the NICU after getting the call our son's lungs were deteriorating. Samuel snoozed through the noise. How could he have slept? His heart monitor read in the 170's. Ralph's forehead wrinkled as he looks at the screen.

The nurse explained morphine was keeping Samuel motionless in order to tolerate the high-frequency oscillatory ventilation (HPOV) machine, which delivers 120 breaths per minute. Part of me wanted to pick him up and run away. I couldn't protect him, but my maternal instinct was on full alert.

A nurse touched my shoulder. "Mom, I'm not sure you know we have a separate area for breast pumping. Would you like me to show you?"

She led me to a separate room with three stalls, each with a curtain. The nurse pulled the first curtain back, revealing a chair next to a machine complete with all the parts I needed. She showed me how to work the device and left. To my surprise, I filled one sixty-milliliter plastic vial. I wrote Samuel's name on the container and took it back to the nurse's station, triumphant in my accomplishment.

The nurse brought a syringe to deliver my milk through a tube going into Samuel's nose to his stomach.

The minutes ticked away.

Ralph pointed to a light on the oscillator.

"Look, Samuel is breathing over the ventilator."

"Okay," I replied. I was puzzled, not understanding the significance.

"And look at this," he pointed to another monitor, "his oxygen level is going up. This is great. I'm going to tell his nurse."

I was confused, not comprehending Ralph's excitement. Just a few days into my son's life, and I'd stepped into a foreign world of machines and medical jargon. There was no handbook to read. No other parents to ask. I was thankful for my husband's engineering background and found myself leaning on him for technical understanding of this new world.

After lunch, Dr. Bravello greeted us by Samuel's pod. He had followed our case since I was on bed rest. Knowing the dire diagnosis we received, he shared his faith and even prayed for Samuel before his birth. His prayers, as a member of the medical community, offered me a ray of hope and encouragement.

He recommended we put a PICC (peripherally inserted central catheter) line in Samuel so the nurses could deliver medicine through a port rather than through an IV. We agreed because it prevented him from being pricked in the foot for a blood draw.

Later I tried the breast pump again. Could my milk have helped Samuel's oxygen saturation to increase? Encouraged by this potential, I produced three vials of milk.

My first Sunday home from the hospital, we went to church. Only a year ago, we had our wedding pictures taken under the outdoor cross. Now I came empty-handed. No fawning over a newborn.

I needed to be uplifted. Singing songs soothed my soul. I drank in the pastor's sermon, enjoying its comfort after so many weeks away.

Before long, my maternal instinct drew me to Samuel like a magnet, and we left church to go to the hospital.

We arrived within fifteen minutes. Dr. Reed approached us. He stopped in front of us with arms crossed. The creases on his forehead made me hold my breath.

"I'm not sure how much hope we can offer in helping your son. He needs high amounts of oxygen and is on a very specialized ventilator. His lungs can only handle so much of the intensity of this machine before they become elastic and nonresponsive."

I gripped Ralph's arm. The nurse called Dr. Reed to help another patient. Why do I think he was glad to be called away?

Dejected, we turned to Dr. Bravello for his opinion. Knowing he was in Samuel's corner, we hoped for better news. To my surprise, he agreed with Dr. Reed's assessment.

Dr. Bravello explained, "Samuel's ribs are hard and fixed, causing his lungs to push into his stomach cavity instead of outward like we breathe."

Ralph countered, "If this is a bone disorder, why don't we break some ribs to allow his lungs to expand?"

I cringed at the thought.

"I don't know if it'll help. We just have to wait and see how he does."

Dr. Bravello left the NICU. We turned to embrace each other.

Each time we arrive in the NICU, we asked the same question, "How is he doing?"

The answer caused me to hold my breath or sigh in relief. Today was no exception.

As we approached his crib, the doctor spoke before we asked, "He's retaining fluids."

My son's face was puffy around his cheeks, and his eyes were swollen. The noticeable change caused me to catch my breath.

Ralph turned to the doctor. "How can you help him?"

"We'll give him Lasix to reduce his fluids and watch for improvement."

"How long will it take to work?"

"Perhaps twenty-four hours."

It couldn't work quick enough for me. I wanted my sweet son's face back to normal.

I settled in a chair next to Samuel's crib, which had a four-inch-high glass enclosure surrounding him in a rectangle shape. I touched his stuffed baby elephant hanging from the overhead light. The bell attached to the elephant jingled. I reached in and moved his brown stuffed teddy bear, laying it next to him. The teddy bear looked huge next to his five-pound frame. Samuel's hazel eyes followed the still-dangling elephant above.

From my purse, I retrieved several three-by-five cards in various colors given to me by my pastor's wife, Marsha. Each card had a scripture verse handwritten on it. I read each one aloud.

"My grace is sufficient for you, for my power is made perfect in weakness. 2 Corinthians 12:9, NIV. He tends His flock like a shepherd: He gathers the lambs in His arms and carries them close to His heart; He gently leads those that have young. Isaiah 40:11, NIV."

Perhaps my singsong voice soothed Samuel, but I found my heart quieted, resting in the words written.

Dr. Davidson called Ralph before I woke about Samuel's genetic test results. He asked to meet us later to discuss the findings. I held on to the belief Samuel had some other diagnosis and not Thanatophoric Dysplasia Dwarfism. I chose to pray instead of worry, though it was a battle.

Dr. Davidson led us to a private room, where we sat at a conference table. He placed a fax on the surface and pushed it to us.

"The blood test shows Samuel has Thanatophoric Dysplasia Dwarfism."

I heard these words, but that didn't make them true. I said nothing, while my mind denied the diagnosis. God is bigger than this report.

Dr. Davidson was a legend at the hospital. He stayed up all night and climbed the stairwell two steps at a time with two Dr. Peppers in one hand and a donut in the other, sprinting between his office and the NICU. Not surprisingly, he found us in the NICU thirty minutes later.

"There's a pulmonologist I think you should talk to—Dr. Lyon. He knows an expert in Texas doing work with these kinds of situations. Perhaps he can find out more for you."

Ralph shook his hand. "Thank you so much for your help."

"My pleasure. Dr. Lyon will be by shortly."

When Dr. Lyon visited, he mentioned the doctor in Texas who could perform titanium rib surgery. However, this specialist had never worked with Samuel's diagnosis. This type of surgery was used more for scoliosis patients.

Even so, hope filled my heart. Maybe this procedure would help Samuel survive.

Chapter 7

PEACE, PATIENCE, AND THE PURPLE CHAIR

*L*ife went on outside the gray walls of the hospital.

Inside the hospital, Samuel's oxygen level was at 50 percent. Knowing we breathe about 21 percent oxygen, it was one step to normal breathing. The staff was comfortable enough with this development to attempt to take him off the oscillator and transfer him to the hospital ventilator.

Earlier a nurse explained Samuel wouldn't come off this highly specialized ventilator, implying he might not make it. Her prediction still rang in my ears.

The plan was once he was off, he would be weaned off the morphine, which was keeping him non-responsive and immobile. I longed to see my son's eyes open again.

At 11:00a.m., the switch was done. Standing next to his crib, I prayed for success. I gazed at each monitor. His little chest rose and fell with each breath. He didn't fight it. The machine took control.

I turned to the nurse looking at Samuel's chart. "How is he doing?"

"So far, so good."

I checked my watch. It was 11:30a.m. I couldn't hold back my excitement. I dialed Ralph's cell phone number.

"Hi, my love. Guess what?"

"Good news, I hope."

"Yes, Samuel is off the oscillator. Isn't that great?"

"Now this is good news. How is he doing?"

"He's still groggy and out of it," I said. "They're going to pull his blood gases to be sure there's no problem there."

"Sounds good, my love. See you soon."

I hung up. *Will the test results show elevated CO_2 in his blood? Or will it be normal? Oh, God, please let it be normal.* I checked on Samuel. Was he dreaming? I looked up at a silent monitor, relieved.

—⟋⟍⟍—

A nurse turned a dial to increase Samuel's oxygen. I saw Dr. Davidson enter the unit and check on another child. As the nurse went to her desk, Dr. Davidson came toward me. He looked at Samuel's chart and made a handwritten note.

"There's a drop in Samuel's red blood cell count. I don't see it as a problem right now, but it's something we need to keep an eye on."

Another request for the prayer chain. I didn't know how a red blood cell count was good or bad but was determined to look it up on the Internet later.

"Oh, okay."

He put the chart down and lowered the dial regulating Samuel's oxygen in an effort to wean him off the high settings. He left the unit.

The nurse chuckled. "You know, Dr. Davidson turns everyone's oxygen down and then leaves. Within minutes, all the alarms go off because the babies can't tolerate the change. So I turn up the oxygen anytime I know he's coming."

I listened but didn't comment. I respected Dr. Davidson because he believed these children could be weaned. He believed in each child and pushed them to their full potential. The goal for every child was to be healthy enough to go home. I understood the nurse's point, as she had to answer all the alarms, but this only increased my respect for Dr. Davidson.

Samuel's nurse leaned on the crib. "Mom, would you like to hold Samuel?"

My heart jumped. "Really? Can I? I'd love to."

I could not hold him when he was on the oscillator.

"Sure, give me a few minutes to set everything up."

She brought in a purple rocking chair and placed it by the crib. I eased into the chair while the nurse disconnected his feeding tube and unhooked the ventilator hose. She gently transferred Samuel into my arms and taped the vent tube to my shirt.

Snuggled in my arms, I marveled as Samuel yawned. Bliss flowed through me. I closed my eyes in thankful prayer. Not wanting to set off any alarms, I kept perfectly still. His eyes closed as I wished for this moment to never end.

Too soon, the nurse swept my son back into his crib. I still felt his weight against my arms.

All was right with the world.

While Ralph was at work, I visited Samuel. Dr. Davidson approached me.

"Mrs. Mann, I'd like to talk to you."

"Of course."

"Your son is relatively stable at this point. However, he isn't able to breathe on his own. If you want to bring him home, he's going to need a tracheostomy."

I turned to Samuel. White tape covered his cheeks. A tube in his throat delivered oxygen to keep his lungs inflated. A tracheostomy would place a tube in his neck. How could they do this? I couldn't see my son's neck because of all his skin folds. His chin sat on his chest.

"There's really nothing else we can do. I need you to sign the paperwork so we can do the surgery."

He paused. I was silent.

"You do want him to go home, don't you?"

I found my voice. "Yes, of course. Can I talk this over with my husband and get back to you?"

"Certainly."

I left the NICU mulling over Dr. Davidson's words. I'd come to trust him as he had advocated for Samuel all along. If having a tracheostomy meant we could take Samuel home, it was worth considering.

———ҳҳ———

I was chatting with my mother-in-law, Peggy, when I noticed Dr. Reed walked into the NICU, bypassing all the other children's cribs, heading directly to us.

"Your son is very critical. Besides needing a ventilator to breathe, his cognitive ability is severely delayed."

I heard the doctor's words and severe tone, but their impact was lost on me. He was explaining facts, but despite the dire prognosis, deep down, I chose not to believe his predictions. The peace I received at the high-level ultrasound in Orlando still rested in my heart. I placed my trust fully on God.

When I didn't respond, the doctor's face turned red.

"Your child will die!" the irritated doctor shouted.

I stared at my newborn as one thought resounds within me, *You will die one day too,* but I said nothing.

Still seeing no reaction, he stormed out of the NICU.

I looked at Peggy. She was silent.

———ҳҳ———

"Dr. Reed told me Samuel has a degenerative brain," Ralph said. "He also said Samuel is going to die."

I frowned. "He told me too."

Ralph reached for my hand. "He also said that he and Dr. Davidson are on the same page about Samuel's prognosis."

I leaned back. "I find that hard to believe. Dr. Davidson's done all he can to help."

"Let's see what happens in the morning."

Waking up, we rushed to make it to the hospital for the morning meeting. As Ralph drove, I closed my eyes but was not able to rest.

Dr. Davidson, Dr. Reed, and a lady from the discharge administration were sitting at a mahogany rectangle table awaiting our arrival. Dr. Reed, being Samuel's primary doctor, started the meeting.

"Thank you for coming this morning. We want to go over Samuel's progress and give you a status update. Though he is off the oscillator, he still needs the ventilator to breathe. The question is, how far can Samuel go? Can he improve beyond where he is now?"

Dr. Davidson chimed in. "Given time, he could improve."

My heart leapt at Dr. Davidson's vote of confidence.

Dr. Reed looked at his colleague. "A week or two will only add negligible improvement."

Listening to the exchange, I realized I was not in control. I turned to Ralph. He leaned forward, both hands intertwined, covering his mouth. He cleared his throat.

"What are you suggesting? What do you recommend?"

Dr. Davidson responded, "Placing a trach could improve Samuel's oxygen exchange."

A ray of hope.

Dr. Reed added, "Yes, that's a possibility. My other concern is Samuel is not gaining weight. He should be gaining an ounce a day."

Ralph shifted in his chair. "He may be five pounds now, but he did get within a few ounces of six pounds at one point."

I chimed in, "Isn't weight fluctuation normal?"

"Yes," Dr. Reed answered. "But he still hasn't gained any weight from his birth, and that's a concern."

I chose not to respond but wondered if he thought Samuel wouldn't grow. I looked at Dr. Davidson; his head was leaned forward, his eyebrows furrowed, but he was silent. Was he holding back, not wanting to upset his colleague?

The discharge nurse piped up, "The nurses came to us asking for us to help you. We know you want to bring Samuel home. We could talk to hospice about your options. They could provide you with nursing care."

We wanted Samuel home but wanted him to be safe. If hospice provided nursing, I was not opposed. I knew his diagnosis meant death bringing, but I didn't believe he was going to die. I know what the textbooks say, but God is outside the parameters of the textbooks.

I spoke, "We're open to help from hospice."

Dr. Reed leaned across the table. "You know, you don't have to go through this."

I looked at Ralph. I hoped he didn't mean what I think he meant. We were not taking Samuel off the ventilator to die.

I responded with a calm, measured voice, "We want what is best for Samuel."

"Then we need to do a tracheostomy," Dr. Reed jumped in.

I turned to Ralph. "I don't feel comfortable with surgery."

Ralph took my hand. "I think we need to do this today. We'll pray before surgery."

I knew everyone was looking at me. Should I step out in faith and follow the leading of my husband or dig my heels in? It was more the unknown I feared. What could happen in surgery? Would this improve Samuel's chances? The doctors seemed to think it was a possibility. I wanted to trust Ralph's instincts too.

I took a deep breath. "Okay, let's do it."

Dr. Reed said, "We'll get everything prepared. Dr. Riley is going to do the surgery. He will meet you before the procedure to go over any questions."

Both doctors stood to leave.

Ralph turned to the discharge administrator. "Our hesitation in doing the surgery this morning is because my wife wants to alert our prayer team at church."

She nodded. "That's understandable. Let's see how things go, and we'll work on the discharge paperwork and call hospice to coordinate."

I placed my hand on the table. "I'll call the prayer chain coordinator after we are done here." Nodding to the administrator, I added, "Thank you for your help."

Stepping into the hallway, I dialed the church prayer coordinator. I pictured Linda's broad smile as I waited for her to answer. I knew she would be able to have the whole church praying for our wee one.

I didn't wait long to share our need. "Linda, can you please let everyone know we need prayer? They are going to do surgery on Samuel this morning to put a tracheostomy in."

"I'm on it."

"Thanks so much, Linda. I'll call you with an update as soon as I know something."

After hanging up the phone, I took Ralph's hand, and we walked to the NICU. I squeezed. He squeezed back. The hand exchange offered me comfort.

We walked into the NICU to Samuel's crib. I looked down seeing tape on either side of his mouth holding his breathing tube in place. What would he look like without the tape? In just a few hours, I'd find out.

I touched Samuel's foot and closed my eyes and silently prayed, "Please, Lord, take care of my son. Guide the doctor's hands. May there be no complications. I can't protect him, but I know you can, Lord. In Jesus Name, Amen."

Ralph wrapped his arms around my shoulders. I didn't cry, but my heart was aching for what could happen.

A man with a white coat came to Samuel's crib, extending his hand to us.

"Mrs. Mann, I'm Dr. Riley. I will be performing the surgery today. Do you have any questions for me?"

His kind eyes put me at ease. He looked to be in his mid-forties and had a genuine smile.

"Have you ever performed a tracheostomy on a child with Thanatophoric Dwarfism before?"

"No, I haven't. I've done many tracheostomies and haven't failed yet."

After the procedure, I saw someone in a white coat turning the corner. I stood up. It was Dr. Riley walking down the hallway.

"How did it go?"

"Your prayers were answered. We successfully placed the tracheostomy, and he's doing well. He'll be brought back to the NICU from recovery in about twenty minutes, and then you can see him."

Relieved, I gave him a hug. "Oh, thank you so much, Doctor."

Ralph and I waited in the hall. After what seemed like a long time, a nurse opened the NICU door.

She waved us in. "You can come in now."

We walked to the crib. The tape on his mouth was gone. I could clearly see my son's face for the first time. He looked beautiful. His eyes opened and looked at us. His tongue felt around the inside of his mouth. How funny. He wanted to explore without the tubes there. I pulled out my camera and snapped a picture. His mouth pursed together, and his eyes shut tight.

"Mom, Samuel's a bit uncomfortable after surgery. We're going to give him some morphine and Ativan to help. He'll be asleep in no time."

I was relieved he'd get to sleep off the effects of surgery. Ralph touched my shoulder. "Let's let them work on Samuel. We need to go see Dr. Parshal. You ready?"

I didn't want to leave but knew he needed to get rest. "Let's go."

We walked across the street to the Doctor's Medical Building and met Dr. Parshal in his office. His heavy Indian accent made him hard to understand. He pointed out a graphics chart of a GI tract.

"This is a picture of a normal GI tract. I need to see x-rays of your son to be sure everything is in the right place. Then I when I do the surgery, I won't get any surprises." He turned to us and smiled. "We will meet again after I get the x-rays."

Chapter 8

A VERY CLOSE CALL

alph came into the bedroom as I opened my eyes to the morning sun streaming through the blinds.

"Did you remember the meeting at church this morning?"

Dragging the pillow over my head, I responded, "No, I forgot all about it."

Ralph pulled the pillow off. "If we leave now, we'll just make it on time."

I opened one eye. "My love, I'm not up to it. Why don't you go?"

He looked into my eyes, testing my sincerity. "I'd rather we go together, but I see you need your beauty sleep. So I'll go."

I rolled onto my elbow and lifted up far enough to offer a soft kiss. "See you later."

I fell back on the bed and once again snuggled under the covers. Closing my eyes, I waited for sleep to meet me. I heard the front door close and realize Ralph had left.

The phone rang and jerked me out of my slumber. How long had I been asleep? I ran past the hallway into the living room and snatched the phone before it went silent.

"Hi, it's me calling for an update." Through my sleepy fog, I realized it was my mother-in-law, Peggy.

"Oh, hi, Mom. Sorry I didn't call. It's been a whirlwind." I sank into the couch. "Samuel is doing good after surgery, though he's a little out of it. They are giving him pain medicine, so he's been sleeping it off."

"Well, I'm glad to hear that. We've been on pins and needles around here. After hearing what the doctor said, I wasn't sure what to expect. Do they really think he's going to have brain delays?"

"I'm so sorry you heard the doctor's prediction. I'm not sure they know what to expect with Samuel. He wasn't supposed to live past birth, and now he has. We are just taking it day by day."

"You're good to take it so well."

I smiled. "We're trusting God with every moment."

"That's good. Keep us updated."

"We will, Mom."

"Let us know if there is anything we can do."

"Thanks so much."

After we said our good-byes, I contemplated Mom's call. She was concerned. This was understandable considering the doctors' prediction that her grandson would die. My heart refused to believe the doctors' declaration, but how would I convince others of my confidence? My peace rested in knowing God is in control even though the circumstances seemed impossible.

I heard the door open, and as I turned, I found Ralph leaning down to give me a surprise kiss.

"Hi, my love. How did it go?"

"Near the end of the meeting, Pastor asked how it was going."

My head tilted up.

"I choked up. My voice quivered as I gave an update, but it was all I could do to speak at all."

I moved across the room. We embraced. No words were needed.

Moving back to the couch, I remembered the phone call.

"Your mom called while you were out."

I shared the conversation. He was concerned enough to call his parents. I could hear only one side of the conversation, but I could tell he was talking to his father. Ralph ended the call.

"So what did he say?"

"Dad asked me many questions, which I tried to answer without getting too technical. Mom told Dad what Dr. Reed said, and he's wondering why we want to bring Samuel home if he's mentally challenged."

My mouth pursed. Ralph nodded.

"I know, I know. I don't think they understand. Mom says she talked to one of our relatives a couple of days ago and was told we should give up and adopt a child instead."

"Well, that's just not going to happen."

"I agree, my love. We just have to be patient with everyone, and we'll keep doing what's best for Samuel."

I exhaled and leaned against Ralph. Closing my eyes, I silently thanked God for such a wonderful husband.

In an effort to discover if Samuel's anatomy would give Dr. Parshal any surprises during the G-tube placement surgery, he gave Samuel a radioactive dye. Though this was not an invasive procedure, Samuel was crying and fussy. Could the infection in his tracheostomy site be the cause?

The nurse continued, "Mom, we're giving Samuel antibiotics to help clear up this infection."

I nodded, happy to know the issue was being addressed. Dr. Kelly picked up Samuel's chart and read the history.

"Mrs. Mann, I have the results from the sonogram and x-rays taken today. Fluid is detected on his brain. However, it does not appear to be an issue right now."

"I'll take this as good news. Will the fluid go away?"

Dr. Kelly placed the chart on the table at the foot of Samuel's crib.

"It could, but it may also increase as well. The area of fluid is stable at this point. It's something to keep an eye on in the future."

"Thank you, Dr. Kelly."

Samuel's fussiness ceased as his eyes closed and he fell sleep. Relieved he was comfortable, I left the NICU and rested on the hallway bench. With no backrest, I leaned forward, resting my elbows on my knees. I was silent, but a prayer flowed from my heart to my Heavenly Father, who knows my son better than I do. A favorite verse came to mind:

> My frame was not hidden from You,
> When I was made in secret,
> *And* skillfully wrought in the lowest parts of the earth.
> Your eyes saw my substance, being yet unformed.
> And in Your book they all were written,
> The days fashioned for me,
> When *as yet there were* none of them.
> (Psalms 139:15,16, NKJV)

This was my hope. Samuel is God's handiwork, and all his days are in His hands.

Sitting at my dining room table, I opened the laptop and pulled up Google. The words of the doctor played through my mind, "Don't research this diagnosis on the internet."

Ignoring the internal playback, I typed "Thanatophoric Dysplasia Dwarfism."

A series of photos appeared. I leaned in closer to the screen. *Is that . . . a baby?* The child's eyes were closed, and her skin was black. There was no life. I closed my eyes, trying to erase the image from my mind. Too late. The picture was forever burned into my conscience.

A website peaked my interest: Little People of America. I called and spoke with the secretary to the medical director, who told me of a sixteen-year-old survivor, but she said the family was very private. She gave me no contact information for them. Why didn't my doctors know of this boy? In awe, I hung up the phone. There was a survivor! And I couldn't even talk to them.

We saw the doctor approach us as we entered the NICU for the night shift. Clearing his throat, he said, "Samuel is having issues keeping his oxygen saturations up. We have tried to suction him several times. His breathing is erratic."

He paused. I exhaled, wondering if I'd be able to catch my breath again.

The doctor's concerned tone had me on edge. He added, "I have arranged for you to have a room in the hospital so you can stay close by."

This sounded bad.

I saw Brittney, Samuel's respiratory therapist, leaning over his crib listening to his chest with a stethoscope as her hand inflated and deflated the AMBU bag.

The alarm above his bed was shrill, causing me to look up. I rushed to Samuel's side and searched Brittney's face for answers. She closed her eyes for a moment. Her eyes fluttered open as Samuel coughed up phlegm.

Samuel turned to me with a huge grin. I heard Ralph chuckle. Relief flooded my body.

Brittney disconnected the AMBU bag, replacing it with the ventilator tubing, and looked up at the now-silent alarm. She turned a dial on the wall.

"He looks much better. So far, he's holding his numbers."

I nodded. "What happened?"

"As I listened to his chest, I heard noises of his airway being obstructed. Then a plug broke loose. Samuel coughed, clearing the obstruction. I turned down his oxygen from 100 percent to 60 percent." She turned to the monitor. "His numbers are holding. That's a good sign."

I hugged Ralph. Smiling, I turned to Brittney.

"Thank you so much."

"Oh, I didn't do anything. I was in the right place at the right time."

"Well, thank God you were here."

Taking a step around the crib, I embraced Brittney. She returned the hug and left the NICU. I never saw her again.

Sleeping in the hospital last night kept us near by after Samuel's close call. But tonight, I wouldn't be sleeping in a hospital room with scratchy sheets and blankets barely covering my feet.

I lifted the phone on the wall by the NICU entrance and told the nurse we were here to visit Samuel. She buzzed us in. The first thing I heard was alarms.

My heart raced as I rushed to Samuel's side and found him completely content. The alarms were not coming from his machines but the crib next to him.

Turning to my right, I could hardly see the wee form of the little girl who was in the next crib. A nurse was manually helping Eleni breathe using the now-familiar blue AMBU bag. The nurse deflated and inflated what looked like a rubber football with a plastic bag on the end. Eleni struggled to maintain her oxygen level in the 80's.

The nurse came to my side and gently asked us to leave the NICU. Stunned by her request, we exited to the hallway. Ralph sat on the bench with his eyes closed in prayer.

I sat next to Ralph. "I don't remember all the visitors being asked to leave before."

Silence fell between us as we contemplated the implications. Taking Ralph's lead, I closed my eyes and prayed for God to touch sweet Eleni.

Ralph reached for my hand. "I don't think they are going to let us back in. It's already 11:30p.m. Let's go home."

In the car, Ralph sighed.

I laid my hand on his shoulder. "You okay?"

"Not really. I am worn-out worrying about Eleni."

"Oh, honey. I know how you feel."

A pleasant surprise awaited us in the NICU. Eleni held her own. What a relief. She's so loved by her parents and grandparents. Their love showed us how to be present and advocate for our son.

Being in the crib right next to Eleni had drawn us close. I joked that Eleni was Samuel's first girlfriend. Sometimes I compared my son's oxygen saturation level with hers. Praying for them both daily came naturally.

My reverie was broken by Dr. Lyon's arrival. He read Samuel's chart, taking a peek at his monitors. Ralph moved to stand next to me.

"I see his oxygen saturations are in the sixties. He is doing good."

"That is good news," I said.

"Perhaps it's time to start trials to move Samuel from the hospital ventilator to the home ventilator."

At the word *home*, I turned to look at Ralph. His eyebrows raised as a smile spread across his face.

I couldn't contain my excitement. "Oh, wonderful!"

"I'll work up a plan to slowly transition Samuel."

Hope surged through me. Could Samuel be on the path to come home? His room was ready, colored in a baby blue with a magnificent mural showing dolphins jumping out of the water.

"We'd love to bring him home."

Dr. Lyon returned my smile. "We'll see what we can do."

As Ralph drove to my C-section follow-up, I reflected on the appointment. Being chauffeured everywhere hadn't been ideal. Hopefully the doctor would clear me to drive again.

After a quick exam and asking me several questions, Dr. Michaels declared, "You are cleared to drive. I would suggest you wait six months to get pregnant again to give your body a rest. You are healthy, and there is no reason you can't get pregnant again."

"Is there a chance I can give birth to another child with Thanatophoric Dysplasia?"

"Since it is a random genetic mutation, I doubt it, but it's not impossible."

"I don't know if I could do this again."

"The chances are very slim and not something I would worry about at this point."

Ralph was silent.

"So let's make your next appointment an annual visit. No need to see me again until then unless something comes up."

Happy I didn't need to come back for another year, I thanked Dr. Michaels, and we left the office.

Once in the car, I turned to Ralph.

"So what do you think about our chances of having a child with TD?"

"The doctor says not to worry about it. I agree. Let's not worry about it."

"But what if it does happen?"

"Then we will deal with it then. If God gives us another TD child, he will help us through it. He sure is watching over Samuel."

Ralph's logic sank into my soul, offering me a peace knowing we were not alone. God was with us. I had a husband who would stand by me and carry the load. I was comforted by his words.

"Then I won't worry about it."

He leaned over the center console and offered me a sweet kiss.

In the NICU, a nurse stepped in front of us. I turned to see Samuel's pod.

"He's doing fine, Mrs. Mann. Can we talk for a moment?"

Without waiting for an answer, she pointed to a desk with two chairs tucked away from Samuel's area.

"Step over here for a moment."

Ralph and I looked at each other but remained silent.

"We are working on Samuel's paperwork so he can be transferred from the NICU to the PICU."

Alarmed, I interrupted, "Why does he need to be transferred?"

"I think you will find the PICU to be more peaceful for Samuel. He will have his own room with a nurse caring for him one-on-one."

"But he has nurses here who know him. I think he'd be better off here."

The nurse looked to Ralph then back at me.

"Well, he can't stay here. This is the neonatal intensive care unit. Samuel is not considered neonatal. He would be at forty weeks gestation if you were still pregnant. Children born at term or older and still need care are seen in the pediatric intensive care unit."

Having his own room instead of all the alarms interrupting his sleep sounded ideal, but I was still nervous about new nurses not familiar with his care.

Ralph asked, "So what do you need from us?"

"There are several papers you will need to sign, including a do-not-resuscitate order [DNRO]. You can specify the type of DNR you prefer. For instance, the DNR could be tailored to be active in case of respiratory failure only or heart failure only or both. In the case of heart failure, the nurse would not push on your son's chest and possibly break his ribs. So it is really up to you."

"Why do we have to sign a DNR?" I realized my voice came across louder than expected.

She sighed. "In order to transfer Samuel by ambulance across the street to the PICU, you need to sign a DNR."

Feeling like we had no choice, I turned to Ralph. "He has such a strong heartbeat. I think we should do it for heart failure only. I would like intervention if he has trouble breathing."

Ralph nodded. "That makes sense to me."

Turning back to the nurse, she held a pen, ready to write.

Ralph, speaking in an even tone, said, "Let's do the DNR for heart failure only. Otherwise, we want all measures taken to help our son."

"I'll have the paperwork ready by tomorrow. The transfer date will be September 17. Do you have any questions?"

How would I ask a question when I didn't even know what to ask? This was unknown territory.

Ralph spoke for us both, tapping her desk. "No questions right now."

Chapter 9

NOT OUT OF THE WOODS

S tanding in line in the Children's Hospital lobby, I waited for the man in front of me to receive instructions to find a patient. Ralph stood next to me looking toward the waiting room. Wall-sized windows allowed sunlight to flood the atrium area, where a children's table and chairs sat in the center. The cushions on an oversized chair exploded with a rainbow of color, adding to the room's happy disposition. A classic red radio flyer wagon sat off to the corner. A toy puzzle covered the sofa table. All these things reminded us we were in a children's hospital.

"Yes, how can I help you?"

"Can you tell me where my son, Samuel Mann, is located? He was transferred from Hamilton Women's Hospital Neonatal Intensive Care Unit to the Pediatric Intensive Care Unit here earlier today."

"One moment. Yes, he's on the second floor." The receptionist pointed down the hallway. "Take the elevator to the second floor. Make a right, then your first left, second door."

"Thank you."

We followed the directions given, then we were buzzed in. The double doors automatically swished open. We stepped into a whole new world. The PICU was laid out in a half-rectangle shape with the nurses' station in the center. A petite woman in light-blue scrubs greeted us.

"Hi, I'm Nancy. I'm Samuel's nurse. Follow me."

As she turned to lead, I could see her brunette hair styled in a tight bun. She opened a bright-red door and entered my son's private hospital room. In the center of the room was a child-sized bed with steel enclosures on each side. Light flooded in the room from two large windows facing the front of the hospital. The bright light greeted me in stark contrast to the darkness and artificial light of NICU. I moved to Samuel's side. His little five-pound body seemed engulfed by the bed. A thin blanket turned into a roll tucked him in on his sides, arms, and legs.

"He's resting well. He must have been tuckered out by the transition."

Once she closed the door, I turned to Ralph. "This room is so full of light. What a difference from the PICU. And he has his own room now."

There was a clear view of the nurses' station through the window blinds. Two nurses sitting at the station were busying themselves with paperwork.

Looking into the crib, I saw Samuel stretch, open his eyes, and smile. I caught my breath at the beauty of the smile. His eyes shifted left then right, looking at his new environment, from a dark, noisy surrounding to a bright, quiet, and sunny room all to himself.

I walked into Samuel's room ready for his second day in the PICU.

I lifted a CD player, placing it on a table by the wall. Hitting play, Bible songs filled the room. I turned down the volume soft enough to hear the "Jesus Loves Me" song playing. I hoped the soothing music would be calming for Samuel.

Ralph opened the box containing Samuel's first bouncer. Anne thoughtfully gave us the gift when he was born. There was no space in the NICU, but here, in his own room, there was plenty.

The nurse watched Ralph emptying the contents. "What are you putting together?"

"A bouncer."

"I'm sure he's going to love it."

Ralph smiled. Before long, Ralph pointed to the bouncer, all assembled, on the floor.

"It's finished."

"Good job, honey. We'll have to try Samuel out in it later. He's fallen asleep."

Even in the hospital, the normal things of life are celebrated, like a baby's first bouncer.

I heard a piercing sound. It was Samuel's alarm. The numbers showed his oxygen level dropping fast. Knowing an ideal oxygen level is between 90 percent and 100 percent raises my anxiety as I saw the digital numbers slide to 85, 80, 75, 70, 60, 50. By now the heart rate monitor was reading 30 beats per minute.

Panic gripped me as a nurse rushed into the room. She looked at Samuel and attempted to assess the problem. Time stood still as I prayed she would do something, fast. Samuel's face was red, and he was crying. Instead of bagging him, she stared at Samuel.

She touched his trach, finding it firmly attached. The wires attached to his chest monitoring his vitals were secure. The ventilator hose was not disconnected.

My brain was screaming, *Do something!* I grabbed Ralph's hand.

The nurse looked at the hoses and followed them to the ventilator. She saw a filter attachment disconnected from the ventilator itself, causing a loss of air exchange to Samuel.

"Oh, here's the problem." She reconnected the hose.

"This happened earlier today too."

My mouth dropped at her comment. Slowly, Samuel's numbers climbed as air was once again pumping oxygen into his lungs.

I was silent. I stroked my son's forehead to soothe him. He stopped crying, though his tears wet the bed.

As she left the room, we heard her mumble, "It's a good thing the DNR order is in place."

Is this why she didn't bag Samuel?

The door closed. I turned to Ralph.

"Did she say she wouldn't have helped Samuel because of the DNR?"

"I think so. I thought the DNR was for heart failure only. He was having an issue breathing here."

I nodded. "I don't want my son to die because of equipment failure."

Ralph whispered, "Let's rescind the DNR as soon as possible."

"There is something else I need to do first."

Opening the door, I approached the nurses' station. "Can you please tape the filter to the ventilator?"

The nurse looked up. "Oh, no can do. Only an RT [respiratory therapist] can touch the ventilator."

"Can you have an RT come to Samuel's room?"

"Right away."

"Thank you."

Stepping back into the room, I updated Ralph on the conversation.

A woman with brown hair walked into the room and used the sink to wash her hands. Once done, she introduced herself.

"My name is Brittney from Respiratory Therapy. The nurse said you wanted to see me."

I piped up, "I would like you to tape the filter attachment to the ventilator."

"I don't know if I am able to do that," she said.

"How can I be guaranteed the hose will not disconnect again? What if someone bumps the hose off?"

"I understand the problem. Let me check into it."

She left the room.

Looking at Ralph, I exclaimed, "Samuel could have died! His heart rate was down to thirty."

"I know. Let me find out how to rescind the DNR," Ralph replied.

Ralph left the room. Relieved not to carry the load alone, I turned back to Samuel. He was asleep now, no doubt worn out by all the stress.

Brittney came into the room with a roll of tape in her hand.

"Had to pull some strings, but considering the hose came off twice today, we're going to tape the filter to the ventilator."

It came off twice?

"Oh, thank you. I appreciate it."

Brittney wrapped the tape around the base of the filter several times and cut the end with a pair of scissors.

"It's that easy. Let me know if you need anything else."

"I will."

Ralph walked in with a corn dog and a slice of pizza from the hospital cafeteria. Pulling a chair next to mine, we sat to eat.

"What did you find out?" I asked.

"I found Dr. Phillips. He said he would have to talk to Dr. Lyon about rescinding the DNR."

"I'm glad we've got the process started."

Ralph nodded. "Couldn't happen fast enough for me."

Finishing lunch, I checked on Samuel. He was still sleeping.

Ralph touched my arm. "I think this is a good time to go home."

A week after transferring to the PICU, we received sad news: an invitation to go to Eleni's funeral. Though I had been to a few funerals, I'd never been to a graveside service. Ralph suggested it would be respectful to attend both events. I agreed, wanting to support Tom and Debbie.

On a partly cloudy day, on September 24, 2005, we drove to the Greek Orthodox church on Swann Avenue. Several men in black suits and women dressed in black dresses walked up to the church entrance. We followed their lead, entering through two ornate doors. The windows displayed scenes from the Bible in stained glass. The mourners were silent, waiting for the service to begin.

Mourners started to cry. As we approached the altar, Baby Eleni lay in her casket, still and perfect. I bent down to kiss her cheek. Samuel's sweet girlfriend.

After the service, we drove to the grave site. Stepping out of the car, I was struck by the peaceful surroundings. The birds sang as the sun peaked between the clouds. The sky met towering trees and an immaculate green lawn. Turning to the right, a lone tent was set up, where a group of mourners gathered.

Walking up the concrete path, we bypassed the tent to visit several nurses we knew from the NICU. They were standing by gravestones of the memorial's tiniest members, children. I overheard a nurse pointing out two of the children. It was eerie to hear the conversation, but at the same time, I was touched by their fond memories of their former charges.

Near the end of the service, the priest encouraged the mourners to find comfort in one another and support the family long after the funeral. To the right, there were several balloons. Tom and Debbie approached the balloons. Unraveling the string, Debbie waited for cameras to be ready and released them all. We watched the balloons mesmerized by their path floating up to heaven.

Enjoying my plate of Chinese food, Ralph said, "It was quite a funeral yesterday. You know the same thing could happen to us." I shot Ralph a look.

"Well, it could."

I frowned. "I don't even want to say it or think it."

Ralph countered, "He's still not out of the woods."

I conceded, "I know."

Ralph's tone softened. "We're still celebrating his monthly birthday."

"I know."

We ate silently. After our conversation, I couldn't wait to see Samuel. I caught myself praying for Samuel as Ralph drove to the hospital. Soon I'd be by his side. My fears calmed when Samuel

Chapter 10

REPORT SAMUEL TO THE ETHICS COMMITTEE?

*D*r. Bravello called a meeting. After some talk of Samuel, he cleared his throat.

"Did you know any member of the hospital can report Samuel's case to the ethics committee?"

I said, "No."

"A doctor, nurse, or even the cleaning lady can go to the ethics committee. Once it is in their hands, the decision to keep Samuel on a ventilator is up to the hospital, not the parents."

As I listened, I remembered a case of a child with TD who was reported to the hospital's ethics committee in Texas. A six-month-old named Sun Hudson was born (September 25, 2005) in Houston, Texas, with the same diagnosis as Samuel. The case was brought before the ethics committee of Texas Children's Hospital, which pushed to disconnect the ventilator, keeping Baby Hudson alive. Lawyers were brought before a judge.

The judge considered a Texas law allowing hospitals to discontinue life-sustaining care, even if patient family members disagree. A doctor's recommendation must be approved by a hospital's ethics committee, and the family must be given ten days from written notice of the decision to try and locate another facility for the patient.

Forty facilities in Texas denied access to Sun Hudson. The Texas hospital supported its decision by stating, "From the time Sun was born . . . he was on life support because his chest cavity and lungs could not grow and develop the capacity to support his body. He was slowly suffocating to death." Texas Children's contended that continuing care for Sun was medically inappropriate, prolonged suffering, and violated physician ethics.

On March 15, 2005, the hospital disconnected the ventilator from Sun Hudson. Soon after, the seventeen-pound boy, held by his mother, took his last breaths. Samuel was born on August 2, 2005.

I didn't know if Dr. Bravello was aware of this case. The possibility of Samuel's case being brought to the ethics committee made me want to faint.

I tried to focus on Dr. Bravello's words. "Perhaps it would be best to continue Samuel's care in a long-term care facility."

I tilted my head. "But what about Samuel not being able to wean off the hospital ventilator to a home-care ventilator? Will a facility have a hospital-grade ventilator?"

"We'll have to find a facility able to accommodate the ventilator Samuel tolerates."

I was still not convinced. "Why can't he just stay here?"

His gentle tone wasn't soothing my frayed nerves. "Understand the hospital's main purpose is to aid and cure their patients. In Samuel's case, some medical staff could say since they can't cure Samuel or aid him in getting onto the home ventilator, their job is done. Samuel not improving also complicates things. As you know, you can't take the hospital-grade ventilator home, so we need to find a facility to take him."

Pressure built in my chest. Coming from Dr. Bravello, whom we trusted and we knew cared for Samuel, it gave his words even more weight.

Ralph said, "So where do we look?"

"There is a facility in St. Petersburg called Florida Sands. And there is a facility in Tampa called Skyfall Pediatric Center. I would visit both and then make a decision. Let me know what you think."

Ralph stood, and we each shook Dr. Bravello's hand. "Thank you,

Doctor, for all the information and your guidance. We'll let you know what we find out."

———m———

Driving alone to work, I contemplated the day ahead. I was going in to the office for a half day. My maternity leave had ended and even though several coworkers donated their vacation time, no time remained. Thinking of not being by Samuel's bedside all day saddened me.

After arriving, I visited Susan, my coworker, at her cubicle. She told me of a dream she had about Samuel.

"Really? What happened?"

Susan pushed her shoulder-length black hair back and swiveled her desk chair toward me.

"I saw you, Ralph, and Samuel inside a circle. You were surrounded by angels."

I pictured the scene in my mind, envisioning Ralph and I looking down at Samuel.

"But the angels are not looking at you. They are faced outward with their backs to you. Their wings were touching each other, and you were completely surrounded."

Bringing my hand to my mouth, I held back a tear. Susan stood, giving me a bear hug, assuring me she was praying for us. Her sweet dream comforted me to believe everything was going to be okay. Going back to my desk, I tucked her words in my heart, keeping my hope for Samuel's life alive.

After work, I headed back to the hospital. Opening the door, I saw the nurse adjusting Samuel's drip feed.

"Hi, Mom." I had to get used to the nurses calling me Mom. I guess it was easier than remembering everyone's name.

"Hi, how's he doing?"

"Great. He has been holding his own pretty well."

"Sounds promising."

"His oxygen saturations have not set the alarm off once today yet."

"That's fabulous."

She smiled. "I'm done here for now. I'll be at the nurses' station if you need me."

"Thank you."

Samuel grabbed a hose and pulled on it. I gently eased it out of his hand. Placing a soft book with a Mylar mirror near his face, he stared at his own reflection. I smiled and wondered if he was trying to figure out who was in the mirror.

Ralph opened the door, surprising me.

"Got off work early. Figured I'd find you here."

He leaned over and gave me a kiss.

"Just in time to hear the good news. Samuel hasn't set off his oxygen alarm today. Isn't that great?"

"Nice to hear."

We both watched Samuel make faces in the mirror.

Reluctantly, I agreed to search for a treatment facility for Samuel. We didn't seem to have a choice. The first facility, called Florida Sands, offered subacute pediatric care. As we drove up to the facility, I braced myself, not knowing what to expect. After realizing there would be only two nurses on duty for the large ward, we decided not to return.

Turning onto the road leading to Skyfall Pediatric Center, a large man-made pond with a water fountain came into view. Two double doors opened to the front office, though not as ornate as Florida Sands, the receptionist's friendly smile made for a warm welcome. Within minutes a woman in nurse scrubs arrived. She introduces herself as Judy and directed us to follow her. We walked down a hallway and passed a large room with several round tables.

Our escort stopped at two blue double doors. She typed a code into a keypad, and the doors opened. She turned to us, explaining, "When visiting your son, we'll give you the password for the day."

While she typed the password, I turned to Ralph with a raised eyebrow. Why would they need such tight security? To keep the children safe?

We stepped into a short corridor with a mural of sea animals painted on the curved wall, making it look like an underwater aquarium. Blue hues of the ocean mixed with coral and swimming fish, much like you'd see in the movie *Finding Nemo*. It reminded me of Samuel's mural in his room at home.

Pushing through a second set of double doors, we stepped into an open area with large windows, which allowed the sunlight to visit the room. As at Florida Sands, I was confronted with children in wheelchairs.

"And this is our nurses' station." She laid her elbow on the flat surface of the chest-high partition. A cup holder was filled with pens and pencils. The chair behind the desk was empty. Papers were piled in several stacks on the desk.

"The nurse on duty must be in a patient's room right now." She turned and pointed to a closed door next to the desk.

"This is our baby room. We have four babies with a dedicated nurse caring for each of them. We don't currently have any space here, so your son will be assigned a regular room should you decide to come here. Here comes Dr. Kelly now. Dr. Kelly, this is Mr. and Mrs. Mann. They are interested in having their son be our newest resident."

Dr. Kelly, stocky, middle-aged, with wisps of grey hair teasing his temples, reached out to shake Ralph's hand. His white doctor's coat was emblazoned with his name over his heart.

"Nice to meet you both." He shook my hand. "So what do you think about our fine facility here?"

Thinking back to the Florida Sands, I responded, "I like the mural in the hallway." I turned to Judy. "And everyone is friendly."

"That's good to hear. Do you have any questions?"

I nodded. "We toured Florida Sands recently. They require each resident to have a DNR in place. Do you have the same policy here?"

"No, we don't require a DNR here."

Relieved, I turned to Ralph as he raised his eyebrows.

Ralph asked, "Our son needs a hospital-grade ventilator called a SERVO-i to breathe. The manufacturer told me the SERVO-i can't be used at home. Is this something you can accommodate here, or would Samuel need to be on a home ventilator to stay here?"

The doctor nodded. "The children on ventilators here use the LTV 950 home ventilator. We don't have a SERVO-i, but I can find out if we can rent one."

Ralph asked, "Can you do it?"

The doctor smiled. "It is unconventional, but yes. If your son needs it, we will do it."

Ralph nodded in approval.

I thought of another question. "How often are you here, Doctor?"

"I'm on call, but on average I'm here every other day unless I'm needed."

"And how many nurses are dedicated to each child?"

"We have two nurses on duty at all times and a respiratory therapist for each shift as well."

For fourteen children? It didn't sound like a good ratio.

I pressed on, "Are parents allowed to spend time with their children? Florida Sands doesn't allow parents to stay overnight. I want to be by Samuel's side as much as possible."

The doctor's eyes narrowed as he crossed his arms. "Typically parents don't spend the night." He paused and smiled. "However, I think we can make an exception here. Now if you don't have any more questions, Judy will take you to registration. There are a few forms to fill out. We should be ready to admit your son in about a week. We will make all the transportation arrangements. How does that sound?"

It was too soon to make a decision, but if we didn't move Samuel, who knows what could happen at the hospital. Dr. Bravello's conversation weighed heavily on my mind.

Ralph nodded. We each shook Dr. Kelly's hand and turned to follow Judy to file the paperwork for Samuel's transfer.

Chapter 11

Becoming My Son's Only Advocate

Skyfall Pediatric Center, October 2005

*W*eather reports warned of Hurricane Wilma approaching Tampa. Looking out of Samuel's hospital room window, droplets of rain fell lightly. No severe weather yet. Not enough to stop Samuel's transfer to Skyfall Pediatric Center.

As a paramedic moved Samuel onto a stretcher, I squeezed Ralph's hand. A nurse disconnected the ventilator tubing while the man in blue overalls connected an Ambu bag to inflate Samuel's lungs manually. As the stretcher wheeled by, I caught up to walk beside my son and hold his hand.

Relieved to travel with Samuel, I climbed into the back of the ambulance. As the ambulance turned onto the road, I noticed the siren was silent.

The rhythmic movement of the vehicle soothed Samuel. He contentedly looked around the interior of the ambulance. The paramedic continued to inflate and deflate the Ambu bag methodically. I sensed the vehicle slow down as we turned into a parking lot.

The back doors opened as sunlight and a cool breeze flooded inside. One paramedic pulled the stretcher toward him as the other continued to give Samuel manual ventilation. Using a side entrance, we went through the same corridor we saw on our tour. Blue painted dolphins were a blur as we passed. I looked back to find Ralph, but he hadn't arrived yet.

A nurse directed the paramedics to the fourth room on the right. Once inside, they gently transferred Samuel to the crib. The nurse turned on the SERVO-i ventilator, checking her chart to be sure the settings were correct. In one smooth move, the paramedic disconnected the Ambu bag while the nurse placed the ventilator tubing onto Samuel's trach.

"How's he doing?" Hearing Ralph's voice, I turned.

Giving him a weak smile, I replied, "He's doing better than I am."

The nurse answered, "Everything looks good. I'm going to do some paperwork. Let me know if you need anything. I'll be at the nurses' station."

I offered her a smile as she left the room.

Seeing a sign on the wall, I pointed it out to Ralph. "Oh, honey, look at the sign." The white cardboard sign with handwritten letters read Welcome to Skyfall.

"Very nice." He turned back to Samuel. "I see they have the SERVO-i. I am glad they were able to rent the equipment."

"Me too." The empty twin hospital bed next to the crib was empty. "I guess Samuel's roommate is at physical therapy."

I heard someone in the hall. It was the cleaning lady pushing her cart. She stopped, stepped toward us, stepped back out, and pushed her cart again. She turned around and stepped back into the room. Looking at Samuel in the crib, she paused.

Raising her head, she cocked it to one side and squinted. "I would never have my child here. I'd do everything in my power so my child would not have to stay in this place."

Was I really hearing this? Why would she make such a statement? We hadn't even been in the facility an hour. Shock prevented me from speaking. Seeing our lack of response, she shook her head and left the room. She didn't even attempt to clean.

Ralph put his arm around my shoulder. I blurted out, "Did we do the right thing bringing Samuel here?"

"Honey, we have no place else to go. Don't worry about her. She's having a bad day."

I wasn't so sure. What did she know that we didn't? We couldn't check out because of what she said, though it crossed my mind. Ralph was right—we had no place else to go.

"I hope you're right."

Ignoring the sinking feeling in my stomach, I stroked Samuel's arm. Perhaps I was calming myself more than my son.

The nurse stepped in the room and adjusted Samuel's ventilator tubing.

"How is everything going?"

Besides the eccentric cleaning lady?

Ralph asked, "Dr. Kelly said I could stay overnight. Is there a cot I can use?"

Her eyebrows furrowed. "Parents don't usually spend the night. We don't have a cot, just the rocking chair next to the crib."

Ralph looked at the chair. He smiled. It was a smaller version of the big purple chair at the hospital. Thankfully, my husband had the ability to sleep anywhere.

"It'll have to do."

As the nurse left the room, Ralph commented, "I want to get to know the staff and have confidence they can take care of Samuel. Hopefully, staying here at night will make us both feel more comfortable."

Wrapping my arms around him, I squeezed tight and whispered, "I love you."

Offering me a light kiss, he whispered back, "I love you too."

Coming into Samuel's room, I found Ralph sitting up in the chair as the morning light streamed through the window.

"Hi, honey, how was your first night?"

He stood and stretched his arms above his head.

"The chair isn't too comfortable. I don't like the alarm system either? When an alarm goes off, the nurse doesn't know where it is coming from. She has to run down the hallway until she finds which patient needs help." I frowned. Ralph continued, "Maybe a baby monitor would work better. I'll bring one in later."

"It's worth a try. Why don't you go home and get some rest? I called the office and told them I'm taking a vacation day. Keep your phone on in case I need you."

"I think I'll take you up on that offer."

Leaning over, he gave me a kiss and a wink.

"See you later."

"Bye, my love."

Seeing Samuel, I had an overwhelming need to hold him. Gently guiding his tubing under my arm, I leaned over and scooped him up. Relaxing in the chair, Samuel settled securely in my arms. He smiled; joy flowed through me as I laughed.

A nurse walked in the room, but I hardly noticed. I focused on getting my next smile. The nurse attached a G-tube to Samuel's belly. I looked up as she poured water into the sixty-milliliter syringe, filling it. My heart raced as I reached out to clamp off the tube, stopping the water. Did she not read Samuel's chart? His fixed ribs pushed his lungs into his stomach cavity. Too much formula or water could cause breathing problems.

I gasped. "You can't give him all that water at once. It could affect his breathing." I checked to see if Samuel's okay. He looked fine, thank God.

The nurse shrugged her shoulders and used the clamp to deliver the water slowly and walked out. Did she think I was an irrational mother? She was probably used to the other kids here who were not as medically critical. I made a mental note to talk to the head nurse.

My mind wandered. What if a mucus plug restricted his airway? Would a nurse be able to respond in time? Suddenly I wished we were back at the hospital, where his room was next to the nurses' station. I wanted to protect my son by bringing him here, but how safe was it? I had to pray and trust God; otherwise, I'd snap under the pressure.

Samuel lay in his crib as the nurse entered the room. I watched her check items off his chart. Touching Samuel's tubing, she saw water pooling in the bottom of the tube. It could be an issue when condensation would form inside the ventilator hose from the humidifier. It was important to shake out all the water from the tubing so it wouldn't choke him. This must be done in seconds as Samuel couldn't be without his ventilator.

I held my breath as the nurse disconnected Samuel's tubing. Furiously shaking the tubing, the water fell on the carpet. Without blinking an eye, she reconnected the tubing to Samuel. No alarms pierced the room. I breathed a sigh of relief.

Though relieved Samuel managed, I was appalled the nurse shook the water on the carpet. She didn't even attempt to dry the floor but instead left the room. This was far from the sanitary conditions of the hospital. The words of the cleaning lady repeated in my mind, "I would never leave my child here."

Driving to Skyfall Pediatric Center after spending a night home alone felt foreign. Ralph and I were living in separate places. When Samuel was at the hospital, he was well cared for. Now Ralph was filling the gap to keep our son safe.

Walking past the seascape mural, I rushed to see my boys. I slipped in the room finding Ralph with his eyes closed, half-slumped in the chair.

I leaned over and whispered in his ear, "Good morning, my love. How'd it go?"

Ralph slowly opened his eyes, stretched, and rose from the chair. "Not so good."

"Why? What happened?"

"Samuel's oxygen level dropped. I jumped out of my chair to bag him. His skin turned a dusty-purple color. I called for help on the baby monitor, but no one came."

I grasped Samuel's crib rail for support. "Oh, no."

Ralph leaned against the wall. "I used the Ambu bag, and Samuel's color came back quickly. He was fine."

I exhaled. "Oh, thank God."

He shook his head. "Then I went to find out why no one responded. I found the nurses' station empty with the baby monitor sitting on top of the counter."

"You're kidding." I slumped into the chair. What could we do? Nothing but pray. Pray for the nurses to be alert. Pray Ralph would continue to fill the gap at night. Pray for Samuel's safety. But for how long?

Pushing through the double doors of Skyfall Pediatric Center, I imagined Ralph asleep in his own bed at home. I knew he needed the rest. I walked down the hall when I heard an alarm blaring. It was coming from Samuel's room. Picking up my pace, I crossed the threshold to see Maria, the respiratory therapist, using the Ambu bag to help Samuel breathe. The monitor showed his oxygen rate increasing with each squeeze of the Ambu bag. I stood frozen watching the numbers increase. The flashing red numbers turned a solid green. Maria disconnected the Ambu bag and then reconnected the ventilator tubing.

Looking up from the crib, Maria wiped her brow, pushing her dark-brown hair from her eyes. She leaned on the crib for support. "Do you know how often I come in here?"

My mouth dropped open. "Uh, no."

She shook her head. "A lot. Too many times to count."

What did she want me to do? I couldn't help my son being medically fragile.

Maria tilted her head. "I am constantly being paged to stabilize your son." Her tone indicated I should do something about it. "I know you have private insurance. All the other children here are under state care."

Her eyes implored me. I suddenly realized she was hinting we take Samuel back to the hospital. Why didn't she just tell me that? Maybe she was trying to protect her job.

I nodded. "I hear what you are saying. I'll talk to Ralph."

Relief spread over her face as she offered me a smile. She turned to put the equipment away and left the room.

Was it possible to go back to the hospital?

The phone rang, jolting us both from a deep sleep. I opened my eyes to see red LED lights from the alarm clock piercing the darkness. It read 5:00a.m. Who was calling at this predawn hour? I heard Ralph speaking. "Yes, I understand. That happens all the time."

After thanking the caller for his time, he hung up, sinking his head back into his pillow.

I leaned on my elbow, adjusting my eyes to darkness. "Who was that?"

Ralph's silhouette could be seen in the red glow of the alarm clock. "It was Eugene, the nurse from Skyfall."

I shouldn't be surprised, but I was. "Why did he call?"

Ralph groaned. "He asked if we know that our son turns blue."

Now I was wide awake. "Really? That's what he asked you? Samuel turns blue all the time."

The bed moved as Ralph sat up. "That's what I told him."

I wanted to crawl under the covers and not come out. "Wow, I'm surprised he didn't know."

Ralph pulled his covers back. "I better go in and find out what's going on. I'll call you at work and let you know what I find out."

I leaned over, offering a quick kiss. "Okay, I'll keep my phone with me."

Ralph sat on the couch watching me pace the living room. Stopping midstride, I threw my hands in the air. "What are we going to do? I know he is not getting the same care as he did at the hospital."

Two nurses for twelve children is not enough care.

I sat next to Ralph. "What about taking him back to the hospital?"

"They don't want him there," Ralph said. "I'll be right back." As he rushed down the hall, I stared out the sliding glass windows pondering what to do.

I knew Ralph was right. The hospital said they were not a long-term care facility. They did not believe Samuel would get better. My brain understood the circumstances, but my heart was breaking. Pressure rose up in my chest at the helplessness of it all. I wanted to protect my son but didn't know how. We couldn't bring him home unless he tolerated the home ventilator.

I wanted to be the good Christian girl and act rightly in all circumstances, but I wanted to yell and scream to let my frustration pour out of me.

I stared at the wooden coffee table in the middle of the living room. If only Samuel could come home. I wanted to fix the problem, but what could I do? With strength I didn't know I had, I lifted the table off the ground, throwing it against the wall. The loud crash brought Ralph running back into the room.

"What was that?"

I didn't say a word. I couldn't. I stared at the broken table. Ralph gazed at me and then at the mess of broken wood at my feet. Tears spilled down my cheeks. He crossed the room in two steps and wrapped me in his arms, cradling my head against his shoulder.

Grabbing a tissue, I wiped away my tears. I looked at the table; my cheeks flushed hot at the thought I broke it.

I sniffled. "I'm sorry."

Ralph picked up a piece of wood. "For the table?"

I nodded.

"Don't worry about it. Things can be replaced. I'm worried about you. We'll get through this."

Touching my chin, he lifted my face toward his and kissed me with such tenderness. I wanted to cry again.

Ralph got up from the couch and picked up pieces of the table.

"You did a good job. I didn't know you were that strong."

I rubbed my nose with a Kleenex. "Neither did I."

He smiled. "It will make good firewood."

I was glad it couldn't be fixed. I didn't want to be reminded of one of my most weak moments.

I sniffled. "I was talking with Susan at work today. She told me she has seen a change in me the last week."

"In what way?"

"Just that I am not myself." I sighed. "I am worried something will happen to Samuel, and I am clinging to my phone all day in case you call."

Ralph nodded. "You seem to be near tears all the time."

I grabbed another tissue. "I have cause to worry, though. I see nurses coming into his room not washing their hands. I'm still upset about the nurse who shook the water from Samuel's tubing on the carpet."

"Maybe we need to suggest that the carpets be cleaned."

I stared out the sliding glass patio doors and began to feel overwhelmed again.

"What is most concerning to me," he continued, "is that the nurses aren't hearing Samuel's alarms. The hallway alarm doesn't work right. I'm not sure the nurses are wearing the baby monitor."

I nodded. "Maria told me she is in Samuel's room constantly. I told her I understood. She said, 'You don't understand. I am in here *all* the time.' Her eyes were imploring me to do something."

"Why don't you call Charlotte and tell her what's happened?"

I hadn't thought of Charlotte, but I should have since she was a nurse at Riverside Metropolitan Hospital.

"Okay, I will call after work and see what she says."

Charlotte was the go-to person at church for all things medical. She prayed for our son when we were pregnant and listened to our questions once he was born.

I pulled into an empty space in the Skyfall Pediatric Center

73

parking lot, turned off the car, and dialed Charlotte's phone number. I shared my list of concerns with her, holding back my emotions, so I presented only the facts.

I paused to allow Charlotte to respond. "Go to the administrator of the facility. Tell them exactly what you told me, as calmly as you told me."

I nodded. "It's taking a lot of restraint not to express how upset I am."

Her calm voice spoke in my ear, "You get more with honey than vinegar."

Getting Ralph on the phone, I shared Charlotte's encouragement.

"Well, my love, go on in. I'm in traffic now, but I'll be there as soon as I can."

"Say a prayer for me. See you soon."

Getting out of my car, I took a deep breath and silently prayed. Stepping into the lobby, I asked the receptionist to direct me to the administrator's office. I knocked on the door and found she was expecting me.

I checked the hallway one more time looking for Ralph, but he hadn't arrived yet.

The administrator folded her hands, asking, "How can I help you today?"

I retrieved my list of grievances and read each one.

- Cleaning lady told us she would never put her child in this place.

- One nurse shook excess water from the tubing onto the carpet.

- Nurses are not washing their hands when they come in the room.

- One nurse called us at home and asked, "Do you know your son turns blue?"

- Respiratory therapist explained how often she was in our son's room to provide emergency care.

- Ralph had to use Ambu bag on Samuel because his saturations were dropping fast. A nurse was nowhere to be found.

- Ralph is spending most nights in the room because we are concerned about the nurses being able to respond in a timely fashion.

I went over each point in the calmest manner possible, willing myself to keep my emotions in check. Charlotte's encouragement to share in a matter-of-fact way kept going through my mind.

Placing the list on my lap, I looked at the administrator squarely in the eye. "I'm most concerned your staff isn't able to handle my son requiring immediate and critical attention."

She nodded. "Would you like us to transport him back to the hospital?"

I thought she would try to talk me into keeping Samuel at Skyfall.

Recovering from my surprise, I found my voice. "Uh, yes. I'd like him to go back to the hospital."

She picked up some papers on her desk. "Then we'll do some paperwork and call an ambulance to transport him back."

I shook my head. "Don't you need an event to happen before the hospital will take him?"

She smiled. "You leave that to me."

Knock, knock. Ralph opened the door.

"Sorry, I'm late. How's it going?"

"Hello, are you Mr. Mann?" Ralph nodded. "Your wife has been sharing your experiences with us this week."

Ralph looked at me with his eyebrow raised.

Still addressing Ralph, she continued, "So we discussed releasing Samuel back to the hospital. Would you be in agreement?"

Ralph sat down. "Yes."

"I'll draw up the necessary paperwork. You can go to Samuel's room and get him ready."

Chapter 12

BLUE ISN'T THE RIGHT COLOR FOR SAMUEL

*I*n Samuel's room, it didn't take long to pack the few items from the dresser into plastic bags. A nurse came in with paperwork for us to sign. She said Dr. Camper had agreed to the discharge.

I handed the bags to Ralph as I heard a knock on the door. A paramedic entered the room, and another one followed behind him wheeling in a stretcher.

The first paramedic stepped toward the crib. "Is this Samuel?

The nurse looked up from her chart. "Yes."

Dropping the crib railing, he said, "We're going to transport him to Riverside Children's. Are you ready?"

I looked at Ralph, who nodded. "Let's do this.

The first paramedic disconnected Samuel's tubes from the ventilator and placed a blue Ambu bag to his trach. The second paramedic gently lifted Samuel onto the stretcher.

Samuel's nurse stepped from behind the crib.

As we left, I wanted to be nice and say something, like "I'll come back to visit," but my heart said no. I knew I wouldn't return.

Instead, I managed to mutter, "Thank you for all your help."

She smiled. "You're welcome."

As Samuel was wheeled into the ER, I heard a nurse talk to the paramedics.

"So what is the patient's status?"

"Transport went fine. We were called by Skyfall to pick him up. He is having desaturation issues."

"Mom, what happened?"

"Uh, he sometimes has problems breathing." I didn't know what to say. It's the truth. Just the other day he was turning blue.

She raised her eyebrow.

"Give us a few minutes to check him out."

I stood back watching a team of nurses, several whom had worked with Samuel before, and a doctor surround him.

"Mr. and Mrs. Mann, I am the doctor on call. I see your son has his ventilator settings on too much volume, up to seventies, when he is used to thirties."

I did not understand the implications of what the doctor was telling us.

"This much volume could cause a lung rupture."

My mouth dropped. How long had the setting been like this?

"His breathing is labored, but the good news is he is breathing over the ventilator."

I asked, "That's great news, isn't it?"

"If he has volumes of fifty or over, he may be able to tolerate the home ventilator. That will be our goal."

Relief filled me—not just because of the good news, but also because we'd have Samuel back in the hospital surrounded by a capable team willing to help him achieve the goal of coming home.

"Thank you, Doctor. We appreciate it."

"We'll complete assessment and then transfer your son to the PICU. I believe that's where you were before."

Ralph cleared his throat. "Yes, that's right."

Shortly after our conversation, we followed Samuel up to his new room, not far from where we were a week ago. Nothing had changed. The night nurse knew Samuel well. Now he was in good hands.

Chapter 13

SAMUEL WILL SURPRISE YOU

*W*e arrived at the hospital the next day and were met by Nora, the hospital administrator.

"Can we talk for a moment?"

Now what could this be about?

Ralph nodded. "Sure."

"We can meet in my office. It's around the corner."

We followed her to a one-room office with a desk and two chairs. We took our appropriate seats.

"Well, what's the plan now?" she said, pen poised to write in Samuel's chart.

My eyebrows furrowed. "What do you mean?"

"I think he should be transferred back to Skyfall," she replied.

Please, Lord, not Skyfall. "That is not an option."

Ralph suggested, "How about we get Samuel on the home ventilator and take him home instead?"

I sighed. So glad Ralph was running interference.

Nora's worry lines creased. "I will talk to the doctors." Her voice wavered, conveying doubt.

"Yes, please," I said.

I knew the care team at the hospital provided constant monitoring with a staff well equipped to handle most any emergency. This was the safest place for Samuel to be weaned off the hospital ventilator. At least for this moment, the discussion was on hold. Perhaps the next conversation with Nora would bring good news.

After lunch in the cafeteria, I realized it was already 2:00p.m.

"Honey, I need to at least make an appearance at work. Can you stay here? I will work for a few hours and come back."

Ralph replied, "Yes, I'll stay with Samuel. See you soon."

Ralph pulled the chair closer to the crib. I dropped the rail even with the crib and settled in the chair. Watching Samuel's many facial expressions mesmerized me. He puckered his lips as if trying them out for the first time. I copied him, doing the same. In a moment, his lips relaxed, and his eyebrows furrowed. I laughed because he looked so serious.

His arms were too short to reach his chin, yet his small stubby fingers attempted to touch the mobile dancing above his crib. I grabbed the stuffed blue dog, placing it close to his chest. He laid his hand on the dog but didn't stroke it.

I heard his tummy gurgle as he tooted at the same time. I looked up at Ralph watching from the other side of the crib. I opened his diaper and discovered what projectile stool meant. Ralph stepped back from the crib as the nurse came into the room. I removed the soiled diaper, grabbed wipes, and did damage control. The nurse rolled up the sheet, replacing it with a clean one.

She commented, "I can see this medicine is not working. I will talk to the doctor about changing the medication to something more gentle. I will see him on rounds tomorrow morning."

"Can you also talk to him about venting Samuel's G-tube to relieve the pressure on his belly?" Ralph asked.

"I'd like to give the doctor the full scope of the problem. I'll measure Samuel's stomach and give the results to the doctor. Then I'll suggest the idea of venting. I also want to talk him about the amount of sedation Samuel is getting. I don't think he needs the sedation as much. I know Samuel does fine without it."

Gladness filled me as I heard the nurse advocate for our sweet son. What comfort to have so many caring for Samuel and wanting the best for him.

The nurse continued, "I will let you know what happens when I see you after rounds tomorrow."

We left the hospital knowing Samuel was in good hands.

"Hi, Mom."

Eventually I felt comfortable with the nurses calling me Mom, but it still felt awkward.

"Hi, how's Samuel doing?"

"Good. We got the dose of lactulose cut in half. He's doing well with it. No episodes so far."

"That's good news."

She smiled. "I also convinced the doctor to allow Samuel to be vented."

Praise God.

"We do it all the time. Venting helps the excess gas to be released instead of increasing pressure in his stomach."

"I'm so glad he agreed. It's hard for me to see Samuel crying."

She picked up Samuel's chart. "The doctor also ordered a change in his feeding. We are going to increase the rate of formula he receives from twenty-one milliliters to forty milliliters."

The look of distress on my face gave her pause.

"Don't worry, we're going to feed him one hour on, two off. Eventually we'd like him to tolerate sixty milliliters, but we'll start with baby steps."

"That makes me feel a little better."

"Dr. Peterson is also pleased with Samuel's progress since his readmittance. He's even directed the respiratory therapist to change the settings on his ventilator from thirty-four breaths per minute to twenty-eight. If he does well, then we'll transition him to the home ventilator."

Though we've wanted this all along, I wondered, were we ready to care for him at home? Would he breathe okay on the home ventilator? Time would tell.

She stepped toward the door. "Oh, I almost forgot, Dr. Peterson wants to have a meeting to go over a plan to bring Samuel home. The meeting is Friday morning, 8:00a.m."

Would Nora be there? Were they going to convince us to send Samuel back to Skyfall? Instead of being hopeful, the fear of going back to Skyfall kept peace far away.

"I'm going to work now. I'll arrange time off for the meeting. We'll be there."

"Good, I'll let them know.

I pressed my lips to Samuel's cheek. "Lord, be with my son and keep him safe."

Finally, I was off for the day. I barely managed to focus at work because my thoughts were with Samuel. Now I couldn't wait to be by his side again.

Suddenly I felt worn-out, having to battle traffic, constant concern over my son, and working again. I silently prayed, opened the door, and took the now-familiar path to my son's room.

Taylor, Samuel's nurse, greeted me with a smile.

"How's did our little man do today?"

The door opened, and Ralph stepped in the room just in time to hear the update. Stepping next to my husband, I gave him a kiss.

"So how's our little man?

Taylor and I laughed.

"What did I say?"

I responded, "That's what I just called Samuel, 'little man.'"

Taylor smiled. "Your little man is doing good. I received an update from the day nurse. She said Samuel had a vent trial today. It started with Samuel getting upset from having a bowel movement."

I hoped her next words were good news.

"He wasn't breathing comfortably on the home ventilator, so he was given chloral hydrate halfway through the test. The medication helped some, but we wanted him to be comfortable, so we put him back on the SERVO-i."

Ralph tilted his head. "Why wasn't the vent trial done with one of us here?"

Taylor picked up Samuel's chart. "Do you want me to make a note only to do the trial when you are here?"

Ralph nodded. "Yes, I would like to be here."

She nodded. "I will let the staff know."

Jotting down some notes, she put down the chart and left the room.

Ralph moved to Samuel's crib and crossed his arms. "Why didn't anyone tell me they were going to do a vent trial today?"

I shrugged.

"I could have arranged to be off work. I'm so annoyed."

"I know, my love. Hopefully it won't happen again. I feel more comfortable with you here. You have a much better grasp of the ventilator than I do."

Ralph moved to my side of the crib. He put his arm around me. "Maybe, but it takes both of us to make this work. You are a wonderful mother."

I returned the hug and smiled. How did I get such a phenomenal husband? In all the busyness of work and having a medically needy child in the PICU, it was nice to hold on to Ralph and let the world stand still, even for a moment.

"Ready to go?"

I nodded.

"Let me walk you back to your car."

He put his arm around my waist and nudged me to the door. I broke lose, leaned over the crib, and kissed Samuel's cheek.

"Mommy loves you. We'll be back tomorrow."

Samuel smiled. My heart burst with joy. I could be content being by Samuel's side forever. Ralph placed his hand on my back, a gentle reminder to leave. I snuck one more kiss and took Ralph's hand.

The hospital conference room had chairs backed up against the walls on all sides. Ralph and I sat down and nodded to the other attendees. We saw Nora, Dr. Peterson, Dr. Lyon, Dr. Bravello, Stella (Samuel's nurse), and Sue (another nurse I didn't recognize).

I crossed my arms, trying to protect myself from what I would hear in this meeting. Running through my mind were thoughts about the ethics committee and what happened to Sun Hudson in Texas. I'd rather be in a dentist chair than here.

The meeting began as words swirled about me. My lips were pursed closed. Normally I was outspoken, often leading meetings, but now when it counted most for Samuel, I was silent.

"You probably aren't going to be able to take Samuel home on the portable home ventilator," Dr. Peterson said.

"So what's next?" Nora asks.

My mind whirled. They were not going to send Samuel back to Skyfall.

"What about bringing the SERVO-i home?" Ralph queried.

Silence.

Dr. Lyon nodded. "Well, the first time they sent the home ventilator in the home setting there was probably a meeting just like this one."

I could hug Dr. Lyon.

"The home health nurses won't know how to use it," Sue said.

"We are willing to learn. We will jump through hoops to make it happen. Besides, it's only a matter of time before Siemens makes a home version of the SERVO-i," Ralph said.

"Do you think Samuel is in pain?" Nora asked.

My mind reeled at her suggestion. I didn't know what point was gained by the question or by how we would answer it. I was fuming inside and chose to let Ralph handle it.

"No, I don't think he's in pain. Does he get upset when he poops? Yes, but other than that, I would say he's happy," Ralph responded.

"What are your goals for Samuel?" Sue probed.

Again, I was floored by the questioning. *Lord, please help this meeting end well. Protect Samuel and help him to come home to us.*

Ralph offered a half smile. "We are planning on enjoying him as long as possible. We want him to have the best care. I believe what has brought Samuel this far is the use of technology, excellent doctors, and our faith and the prayers of others."

Dr. Lyon said, "There were days in the NICU we didn't think Samuel would make it. And he's still here."

Dr. Bravello nodded in agreement.

I smiled. They saw how far Samuel had come.

"The hospital is not a risk-free environment," Dr. Peterson offered.

Ralph countered, "Any life is not risk free. My friend had three car accidents recently."

How would you answer that one? No one tried. Since no one was speaking, I decided it was time for me to give my opinion.

"I know I have been silent for much of the meeting, which is unusual for me. Just ask my husband." Ralph smiled and nodded. "But I want it known we will not consider returning Samuel to a long-term care facility. I won't say anything more on that subject because it will only upset me."

After not speaking the whole time, I was surprised by the intensity and force in which I used my words. That was how strongly I felt about Skyfall, but I didn't expect to come across quite so forceful. Ralph picked up on my tone, perhaps surprised himself.

Ralph interjected, "We felt as if we were walking on eggshells the whole time we were at Skyfall. Our primary fear was that with one missed alarm, we would have a dead baby on our hands."

Everyone looked down at their hands. Point made. We were not going to Skyfall again.

Ralph continued, "I know where you can find a couple of SERVO-i's though," referring to Skyfall.

Dr. Lyon's lilting accent calmed me despite the subject matter. "The insurance company will not consider the higher cost to rent the hospital grade ventilator." Pausing, he twirled a pen in his hand. "Perhaps they will compare the cost of being in the PICU against being at home and approve the cost. You still have to overcome wiring the home for the vent and the potential code requirements."

Ralph smiled. "Let me work on getting the unit up to code."

Ralph must be thinking of his years of working with regulatory agencies in his job in the hazardous waste business.

Dr. Lyon grinned. "Why do I think when I'm in my seventies, looking back over all my patients, I'll be writing about Samuel?"

The thought warmed my heart. Out of thousands of patients, it was my miracle son who inspired this doctor.

Ralph turned to me and smiled.

I cleared my dry throat. "Oh, and one more thing." Everyone turns to me. I raised my finger in the air. "Samuel will surprise you."

The doctors got up to leave. Did I see a hint of acknowledgment in my statement, or did they think I was holding on to hope for hope's sake?

Catching up to Dr. Bravello in the hallway, we thanked him for coming. It was so good to see him and have someone we know was an advocate for Samuel and believed in him in the meeting.

Walking into Samuel's room, the nurse smiled as we entered.

"Dr. Peterson has given orders for another vent trial. We're going to set his O_2 not to exceed 40 percent for the test."

"Is that good?" I asked.

"The more we can lower the amount of oxygen he needs, the less oxygen you'll need to have him on when you take him home."

Ralph nodded. "That makes sense."

"He will still get chloral hydrate. It will keep him calm for the test."

I wanted Samuel to be comfortable, so I didn't protest the drug. I was praying he wouldn't need it for the next trial.

"How long will he be on the home vent?"

"That depends on how Samuel handles the change. I overheard the doctor say he would be surprised if he lasted longer than fifteen minutes."

My speech about Samuel surprising them hadn't sunk in yet.

"I'm waiting for the medicine to be drawn up. I'll be right back."

I turned to Ralph. "I hope Samuel does better on this trial than the last one. Then they can be surprised." I smiled.

Ralph replied, "Dr. Peterson told me yesterday that the machine was shoving breaths into him after he breathed over the ventilator, so he wore out quickly. I'm thinking he's going to change the settings to be more gentle."

The nurse walked in holding a syringe. "Here it is. I'll give this to Samuel. RT should be here in a minute with the home ventilator."

I silently prayed for everything to go well.

RT arrived. He turned to Samuel's nurse. "Dr. Lyon ordered for the test not to exceed 40 percent oxygen."

Ralph looked at me and smiled. I smiled back. I whispered, "He'll surprise you."

The sedation made Samuel's eyes heavy as his mouth fell open.

The RT switched machines. I check the clock; it was 11:50a.m. The monitor above Samuel's crib read 98 percent oxygen. Great. Now if he could keep it up.

The room was quiet except for the swooshing sound of the ventilator. Even the alarms held their sound. Samuel's breaths were soft and even. Perhaps the settings on the home ventilator were changed to better sense Samuel's breaths.

The RT approached Samuel's crib. "Mom, we're going to take a blood gas. I'll try not to disturb him."

I didn't know how being pricked with a needle in your toe would not wake him up. I didn't want him to cry and get so upset it would end the test. *Dear Lord, please intervene.*

He pricked Samuel's toe, but I didn't hear a cry. The RT took the sample and left the room. Samuel slept through it all. The test continued. I was amazed and relieved at the same time.

As Samuel still slept, x-ray technicians arrived to take pictures of his chest. One tech slipped a film under him while the other swung the portable machine over the crib. A couple of clicks, all done.

The nurse came in with a clipboard. "Samuel's doing great. We received the results from his blood gasses, which are in the normal range."

Oh, good. In the NICU, that was a problem. He wasn't exhaling CO_2 properly, so it was building up in his system, which could have caused respiratory failure.

Ralph said, "That's good news. Since everything is going great here, why don't I drop you off at work?"

I wished I could spend the day with Samuel, but I needed to go to work. Reluctantly, I agreed.

Ralph navigated the three-mile drive to the hospital with ease. Missing the rush-hour traffic was a blessing.

We arrived in Samuel's room as the RT was wheeling the home ventilator toward the door.

The nurse turned and smiled. "Samuel just finished the trial."

I turned to Ralph and whispered, "So much for the test only lasting fifteen minutes."

He looked at his watch. "It's been more like four hours."

The nurse chimed in, "Dr. Peterson lowered a setting on the ventilator about the same time Samuel decided to have a bowel movement. It was not a good combination. To help Samuel recover, we took him off the home ventilator."

I came close to Samuel's crib. He was breathing well and on his side, reaching for his Mylar mirror.

I looked at Ralph. "I guess Dr. Peterson didn't know about Samuel's tantrums when he has a poopy."

"I guess not."

I clapped in delight. "He lasted four hours on the home ventilator. Isn't that awesome?"

"Yes, my love, it is. Your statement about how Samuel will surprise you came true."

I smiled. "Yes, he will." I asked the nurse, "Can you help me? I want to hold him."

"Oh, of course."

I grabbed the purple rocking chair by the crib as the nurse got in position to pass Samuel to me. She tucked his ventilator tubing under her arm, leaned over, and scooped him into her arms. She turned, gently laying my son into my outstretched arms.

The swoosh sound of his ventilator faded away. His face turned to me. I bent my head to kiss his forehead. His hand touched my face. I looked up at Ralph, who was grinning at the sight of his wife and son together. Pure peace, for this moment.

I was so looking forward to being with Samuel. Ralph drove me to the hospital to drop me off so he could go to church to help set up for the Fall Festival activities.

Ralph turned to me at the stoplight. "Today is the day Samuel will be on the home ventilator without any sedation."

"I am so excited he was on the home vent for four hours."

"Did you hear what Dr. Lyon said?"

"No."

"He said, 'Again, my crystal ball was wrong.'"

Imagining Dr. Lyon painting an image of a crystal ball with his hands, I chuckled. "That's great."

"I thought so too."

Ralph brought the car to a stop at the hospital entrance.

"I'll see you after I help out at the church. Call me if anything comes up."

He leaned over, offering me a light kiss.

"I will."

I checked in at the reception desk for my hospital pass and took the elevator up to the second floor. The nurse buzzed me into the PICU.

Samuel's nurse greeted me from the nurses' station. "Hi, Mom, we're about to start the test."

"Great."

"Suzette just brought the LTV into Samuel's room. Let's see if she's ready."

I followed the nurse to Samuel's room. Suzette was connecting hoses to the LTV. She turned to greet me.

"Hi, Mom. We are getting ready for another trial. No sedation today, and we're going to keep his oxygen at 40 percent."

Samuel lay in his crib oblivious to the changes that were about to occur. I reached out and tickled his belly. A grin spread over Samuel's face. In seconds, a full smile lit up his whole face. Joy filled my heart.

"Okay, Mom. Here we go."

Suzette held the tubing to the LTV in one hand, disconnected the tubing attached to Samuel's trach, and swapped it out in one swift move. Samuel blinked a couple of times, but there was no other reaction. Suzette waited a full minute. She pushed a couple of buttons on the SERVO-i, rendering it silent. She looked at Samuel then at the LTV.

"Everything looks good. I'll be back in a little while to check on him."

I smiled. "Thank you, Suzette."

The nurse picked up Samuel's chart, making some notes, I assumed, about the transfer of vents.

"Mom, I'll be right here at the nurses' station if you need me."

"Okay."

Pulling up a chair to the crib, I pushed my hand through the iron slats and touched Samuel. Tucking my finger in his pudgy, web-like hand, he wrapped his hand around my finger. I marveled at his soft skin. All his fingers weren't able to encircle my index finger. Samuel used his other hand to touch his chin because his arms weren't long enough to reach my hand.

I stood up, leaned over into the crib, and kissed his forehead. "Mommy loves you, Samuel."

Humming the tune of "Jesus Loves Me," I stroked his arm. I didn't know who was being soothed more, Samuel or his mommy?

Ralph came back to pick me up after being at the church.

Ralph reached for the phone, dialed the hospital, and waited for an answer while I went into the kitchen to make a cup of tea to go.

"Okay, my wife will be there soon. Thank you for the update."

Ralph hung up the phone.

"What did they say?"

"He was on the home ventilator all night."

"Wow. That's awesome."

In Samuel's room, the LTV vent sent a shrill sound throughout the room. The machine read Low Minute Volume in red LED lighting. If there was a leak somewhere, if more air was being expelled around the tracheostomy through Samuel's mouth or nose, this alarm would sound. The noise startled Samuel. The nurse came in, read the alarm code, and left the room. I could hear her calling for a respiratory therapist from her station.

I dialed Ralph's number. He picked up on the second ring. "Hi, honey, everything okay?"

"Yes, but there's an alarm going off on the ventilator. I'd feel better if you were here. Can you come to the hospital instead of going to church?"

"I'll turn around right now. See you in a few minutes."

The respiratory therapist entered the hospital room, silenced the alarm, and picked up Samuel's chart.

"He's been on the home ventilator for twenty-two hours now."

Pride welled in my heart at the news. He had been on the home ventilator much longer than the fifteen minutes predicted the other day.

"I'm going to transfer him back to the SERVO-i to give him a chance to rest."

I nodded in agreement. No reason to push him to the point he would get worn-out.

He turned on the SERVO-i, swapped the LTV hose with the

SERVO-i hose, and paused, looking for Samuel's reaction to the switch.

His little chest rose and fell with each breath delivered by the hospital vent. The respiratory therapist nodded and turned off the LTV.

Ralph rushed in the room. "How is he?"

"He was just switched onto the SERVO-i. The alarm stopped, and he's not fussy right now. He was on the home ventilator for twenty-two hours."

"I'd say that was a successful trial."

I smiled. "One more step to bringing Samuel home."

Ralph wrapped his arm around me, giving me a side hug. We watched Samuel fall asleep as he allowed the ventilator to breath for him. When would we be able to bring our son home to sleep in his own crib without the sights and sounds of the hospital? Soon, hopefully, very soon.

—✴—

Dr. Johnson stood by Samuel's crib. "Would you like to see an x-ray of your son?"

Ralph and I followed him to the nurses' station. He touched a few keys and swiveled the computer toward us. I tilted my head to look more closely at the image. The screen showed a chest x-ray with perfectly defined ribs. The ribs reached the entire chest wall, and the rib bones were thin. Though not an expert, I thought the x-ray looked great. It looked normal to me. Relieved, I wondered why the doctors were concerned about Samuel.

"This is a picture of another child. As you can see, I've blocked out the name for privacy reasons."

I thought this was Samuel's x-ray.

"See the clearly defined ribs here." Dr. Johnson touched the screen. "This is what a normal child's x-ray looks like."

Turning the screen back, he tapped the keyboard a few times and turned the screen back to us. "This is a picture of your son's x-ray."

The difference was stark. Samuel's ribs looked much thicker, barely reaching to the outside of the chest wall. The ribs looked almost half-formed, not fully curving to center.

Dr. Johnson looked up at us, smiling. "The x-ray I see here does not match the smiling child I see before me."

My smile grew. Yes, his not-compatible-with-life diagnosis did not match the contented, happy son lying in his crib bed in the PICU. I saw this truth, and now so did Dr. Johnson. One victory, one person at a time.

Turning back to the x-ray, he pointed to Samuel's ribs again. "I do see some slight deterioration where his lungs are losing elasticity in the alveoli. I would like to lower the PEEP settings on his ventilator to compensate."

I knew enough medical terminology to understand the PEEP, positive end-expiratory pressure, was what was keeping Samuel's lungs inflated so they wouldn't collapse. Reducing the PEEP worried me, but as long as there was enough pressure to keep the lungs open, then the job was still done. It should avoid Samuel's lungs from losing their elasticity, which concerned the doctors when he was on the oscillator.

Ralph nodded. "That makes sense."

"I will let respiratory therapist know to make the change."

Chapter 14

107 Days Feels Like A Lifetime

ntering the lobby, I wondered how many times we'd have to come here until our son was home. The guard nodded and handed us our badges. We were the regulars, the ones who always showed up. Most patients would stay just a few days, a week or two at the most. Today was 107 days. Seemed like a lifetime.

"Just remember, he'll surprise you," I told the doctors. Where did that confidence come from? Experience and an abiding faith in the God, who gave me the peace that passes all understanding. Where did my peace come from? "My peace comes from the Lord," the psalmist wrote. Those words were my hope.

We passed a team of nurses and Dr. Sanchez exiting Samuel's room. Samuel's eyes were squeezed closed as his arms move up and down. He was grunting like he was trying to poop again.

Samuel's nurse, Sy, stood by the crib. "He's been fussy this morning. Though it looks like he's trying to have a bowel movement, it seems to be a respiratory problem," she said. "His saturations are lower than we like, so Dr. Sanchez suggested we find a new trach with a longer extension. One of the nurses is looking for one now."

Looking at the dial behind Samuel's crib, the monitor showed the amount of oxygen going to the ventilator was set at 40 percent. The alarms were quiet because they'd increased the oxygen flow. Reaching into the crib, I stroked Samuel's arm and leaned over to whisper in his ear, "Hi, my love. Mommy's here."

I kissed his check. No change. *Oh, Lord, please help them find the new trach.* My heart pounded in my chest as I stroked Samuel's side over and over, hoping my touch would calm him. Ralph placed his hand on my shoulder, offering me the comfort of his presence.

A nurse entered with a small white box in her hand. "Found it."

Oh, thank God.

Sy approached the crib.

"Mom, we're going to do a trach change. We will take the Shiley Samuel is using out and put this new trach in." She lifted the white box in her hand. I stepped away from the crib to allow the other nurse my space to assist in the transfer.

Sy lifted Samuel up into a sitting position. The other nurse opened the box and pulled back plastic cover, releasing the new trach free. Opening a tube of lubricant, she coated the tip of the trach. Sy released the Velcro strap and held the trach in place. "You ready?"

The nurse nodded.

I closed my eyes. I couldn't watch.

"All done," Sy said.

I opened my eyes. Samuel was laying back down. His arms and legs weren't thrashing. The grunt noises were replaced with silence. As the assisting nurse stepped away, I took her place. Samuel looked at me and smiled. *Thank you, Jesus.*

Ralph shook his head. "What kind of trach did you use?"

Sy picked up the box. "It's a flexie Bivona. This one was a special order which was never used. The part of the trach in Samuel's neck is longer than a regular flexie Bivona." She looked at Samuel. "He sure does like it."

"Thank God it worked," I said.

Ralph picked up the box. "The trach tube is 4.0 millimeters. Wasn't the Shiley 4.5 millimeters?"

"Yes, but this one can be inflated to 5.0 millimeters if needed. It's also kind of expensive. Without modifications, it's $900.00."

I was hearing Ralph's conversation with Sy, but I couldn't help but stare at Samuel. He was so uncomfortable. Now he's 100 percent better.

Ralph followed my gaze. "I'm amazed such a little change can make such a big difference."

Tony, the respiratory therapist, entered the room. Sy gave him an update. He nodded and turned the oxygen dial from 40 percent to 35 percent.

Dr. Peterson arrived, stood at the end of the crib, and paused, looking at Samuel. "He looks much happier now."

I nodded. "I know. I can't believe changing this trach made such a big difference."

"Why don't we let him get used to this trach for a little bit and then try him on the LTV again?"

Seeing Samuel so happy, could he now tolerate the home ventilator?

Dr. Peterson followed Tony out of the room, promising to return for the trial.

Tony was setting up the LTV when we arrived after a quick lunch. Samuel's contentment continued as he played with his mirror. We stood by the crib, leaving Tony enough space to work. He turned on the LTV and lifted the tubing, laying it in the crib.

I held my breath. Would Samuel get upset? Would he notice a difference? Would he have to go back on the hospital vent, making our quest to bring him home seem even further away?

With one swift move, Tony disconnected the SERVO-i tubing and replaced it with the LTV tubing onto the trach. He paused, listening for Samuel's breathing.

We all watched Samuel's chest rise and fall. The pattern was even.

Tony turned off the SERVO-i and marked the chart. Sitting in the purple chair, I relaxed for a moment, thankful for a smooth transition, as Ralph stood next to the crib. Several moments passed, and all was quiet.

Ralph broke the silence. "Honey, I think Samuel is trying to poop."

I jumped up, rushing to the crib. Samuel was wiggling side to side with a face full of stern concentration. An alarm pealed out its message, demanding attention. Tony stepped over to the LTV, silenced the alarm, and stared at the display settings.

Ralph joined Tony by the vent and asked, "Are you sure the vent settings are set the same way from the last trial?"

"Yes, of course," he answered curtly. "Anyway, there's no difference in performance between these ventilators."

Ralph gave me a look of doubt. If that was true, why couldn't he tolerate the home ventilator? I saw Ralph's face, but I was still trying to calm Samuel down by stroking his body.

Samuel's nurse rushed in with Dr. Peterson following close behind. Tony gave Dr. Peterson a synopsis of events while the nurse came to my side. I heard Dr. Peterson discussing with Tony whether to increase Samuel's oxygen or end the trial by placing him back on the SERVO-i.

Dear Lord, just do something.

Ralph expressed his thoughts that the LTV settings need to be tweaked.

To my relief, I heard Dr. Peterson pronounce, "Just put him back on the SERVO-i. And get the manufacturer's rep in here," before he stormed out of the room.

Ralph's broad grin looked like he just scored a victory.

Tony, putting down his chart, reconnected Samuel to the SERVO-i.

As much as I wished Samuel wouldn't need the hospital-grade ventilator, I was glad we had the option to make him feel better. The change in him was almost instantaneous. His face relaxed as his chest rose and fell in rhythm, but he was still squirming. At least he was letting the vent do the work of breathing for him.

The nurse checked his diaper. Finding results, she changed his diaper.

The squirming stopped. I didn't know who felt more relieved, Samuel or me.

All was calm again. No alarms and a child falling asleep. The in-and-out swooshing sound of the ventilator filled the room like background elevator music. I sat back in the purple chair while Ralph stared at the LTV ventilator Tony left behind. Hanging from the back of the ventilator in a plastic sleeve was a booklet. Ralph pulled it out.

Muttering to himself, he said, "It's the manual."

Pulling up a chair next to mine, he leaned over to me. "I find it hard to believe the settings on the SERVO-i are the same as the LTV. Maybe I can find out if I read the manual."

I nodded. He turned the pages, reading silently.

Stepping into this medical world overwhelmed me. Most times I was just holding on, trying to understand all the terminologies. As I watched Ralph read the LTV manual, I was so thankful for a husband who was not intimidated and willing to conquer whatever was thrown at him. Ever the problem solver with an engineer background, I pondered if God didn't bring us together for such a time as this.

—⁓—

Numbers vied for our attention: CO_2, pulse ox saturations, temperature, and heart-rate readings. They documented Samuel's efforts to stay alive. We didn't know the outcome but were resolved God was in control. Each LTV trial was one step closer to our goal to bring Samuel home.

I noticed brightly colored paper leaves on the wall as I walked to the elevators in Riverside Children's Hospital. The fall decorations reminded me of the upcoming Thanksgiving holiday. Celebrating it was the furthest thing from my mind. My only thought was to visit Samuel during my lunch hour. Inside his room, Ralph was standing by the metal-railed crib.

I gave Ralph a quick kiss. "How did Samuel do on the LTV trial?"

"Samuel lasted for two hours, but he didn't do too well. The nurse took a blood gas and found out his CO_2 is high."

This was not good. His lungs needed to release CO_2 and not allow it to elevate in his little body. Either the pressure, amount of air the ventilator was delivering, or the breaths per minute needed to be adjusted by the respiratory therapist. Our therapist this week was Darlene.

Ralph lowered his voice to a whisper. "I'm frustrated Darlene changed Samuel's settings. She told me Samuel is a special case and his trach is different."

"Why doesn't she use the settings from the test that worked?"

Ralph shrugged his shoulders. "She keeps getting called away to other patients. She can't even stay long enough to make adjustments."

Dear Lord, please intervene. Help Samuel get on the home ventilator.

Ralph cleared his throat. "Another issue came up this morning. Samuel's nurse, Zoe, told me I'm not allowed to touch Samuel's oxygen button."

I closed my eyes trying to remember which nurse was Zoe. A picture came to mind of a nurse, maybe late twenties with straight cropped black hair framing her oval features, with a smile never quite reaching her eyes.

His voice was raised. "My blood pressure went up when she told me."

Telling my husband *no* or *can't* is the fastest way to see the veins on his forehead pop out. Raised believing anything is possible, he would attack every problem with a can-do attitude. So telling him not to fix Samuel's oxygen level had him muttering a familiar verse, "The wrath of man worketh not the will of God."

"Why not? We do it all the time. Other nurses told us to adjust the setting when Samuel needs oxygen."

We spent many hours with Samuel in a little over four and a half months. We watched the nurses providing care, and after a while, they trusted us to help. Often times they were helping other patients. If the oxygen level in Samuel's body decreased, an alarm would pierce through the room. We'd adjust the oxygen control like we were shown, which would silence the alarm.

Ralph nodded. "I know, but Zoe reported it to Dr. Thomlinson, and he paid me a visit. He said the staff is supposed to oversee Samuel's care, not the parents. He instructed me to press the call button if Samuel needs help." Ralph raised one eyebrow and shook his head. "So when he turns blue, I'm supposed to hit the call button and hope someone comes in time to help? He went on to say our help is a liability for the hospital." He paused and lowered his voice. "And having a child turning blue isn't?"

My husband was not often given to drama, so I knew he was steaming. "So how did you leave it with him?"

"I told him I would follow whatever policy was in place. I don't agree, but I was nice enough about it. And he said you can't touch the equipment either."

Would I be able to restrain myself if Samuel needed help? "As long as a nurse comes to help, I'll comply."

Ralph looked at me knowingly. "Um-hum."

I gave him a coy smile. "I will."

"Apparently, the good doctor told Dr. Lyon and Dr. Bravello of our extracurricular activities too. I heard through the grapevine we're not the first parents who had a run-in with Dr. Thomlinson. I'm not happy."

"I can see why. Remember, we need to love the doctors too."

As a Christian, we are to love others even when they are acting unlovable. It'd be easier to love the doctor, once Ralph calmed down.

Ralph continued, "That's not the only issue. Samuel is having bradycardia events again and is desaturating more often."

I pondered the ramifications. A low heart rate, otherwise known as bradycardia, prevents the brain and other organs from not receiving the necessary supply of oxygen. The oxygen decrease (desaturation) causes the alarms to blare, requiring intervention by piping in added oxygen through the ventilator.

I shook my head. "This is why we should be allowed to intervene. If a nurse is busy, I need to be able to increase Samuel's oxygen."

Ralph placed his hand on my shoulder. "I know. Let's pray that never happens. In the meantime, we'll agree to allow the nurses to adjust the settings on the machines."

I looked down at my hands, not sure I could agree. Despite my misgivings, I squeaked out, "Okay."

"Oh, I almost forgot to tell you. I saw Dr. Lyon today. He asked me how I thought the LTV trial went yesterday. I told him I felt it wasn't a good test and suggested Suzette perform the next test. I know she'll devote her full attention to Samuel. Dr. Lyon thought it'd be good to give Samuel a break, so he will stop testing for two weeks."

Maybe Samuel needed a rest, but at the same time, I wanted him to come home. It was more important he come home when it was the right time. Emotionally torn, I had to trust God's got it all together.

"I hope Suzette is available when they do the test again." I reached for my purse. "Honey, I've got to get back to work. My lunch break is almost over, and I don't want to be late."

I rushed back to work, weaving in and out of traffic to make it to the office on time. Though my boss knew where I went on my lunch hour, I didn't want to take it for granted. Once I was settled in at my desk, I struggled to focus on the long list of tasks at hand. I kept my cell phone with me at all times, just in case I received a call from the hospital. I was ready to go at a moment's notice. Being so close to the hospital has its benefits. I was also thankful for my 6:30a.m. to 3:30p.m. shift, allowing me to escape most of the rush-hour traffic.

Once at the hospital again, turning past the nurses' station, I saw a man in white doctor's coat with a medium stocky build and dark-brownish black hair exiting Samuel's room. I recognized Dr. Thomlinson as he walked away from me, but he stopped upon seeing me approach.

"Mrs. Mann, did your husband talk with you about our conversation this morning?"

I nodded and entered into Samuel's room. I'd rather not have this discussion in the hallway. "Actually, he did."

"So you do understand either you or your husband are not to touch the equipment but to allow the nurses and the respiratory therapists to manage the equipment?"

I responded, "The nurses encouraged us to make adjustments if they were busy, but yes, we will comply with your request. You may want to advise the nurses of the change as well."

I chose to not to make an argument about whether the nurses

were always available. I agreed with my husband; I'd have to pray about that one. He nodded. "I will let them know."

Pushing his eyeglasses up, he reiterated, "As long as you don't touch the equipment, we'll be fine."

Thanksgiving passed uneventfully. With our focus being solely on Samuel, we didn't have the family over for a huge Thanksgiving meal. Thankfully, Ralph's brother hosted us, which allowed us to go back to the hospital after dinner.

After getting good news about Samuel progress yesterday and seeing his weight chart, I was encouraged for Samuel's hearing test today. The only issue we noticed was when he was on a vent trial, his weight would decrease. Because he had to work harder to breathe on the home vent, Ralph felt the machine was beating him up, causing problems like bradycardia and desaturations.

The nurse gave Samuel Valium and chloral hydrate as a sedative for his hearing test. Though this would have knocked me out, our son was more interested in studying the new wires and probes attached to him. The nurse giving the test raised her eyebrows and threw up her hands. She left the room hoping he'd be asleep so the test could go on. She asked the nurse on duty to page her when our son's eyes closed for his nap.

Later we found out Samuel's left ear hears better. Volume had to be increased to hear lower frequencies. Both ears were registering below-normal levels. She said a desaturation could have killed some of the sensitive hearing cells or some of the medicines he received in the NICU.

Though I should be upset by this news, I focused more on the miracle our son was doing so much better than any doctors ever imagined. Keeping him alive was priority. It never occurred to me to ask about the drugs they were administering or their side effects.

After the test, the nurses gave Samuel a soothing bath to remove all the residue the probes left on his sensitive skin. Though Samuel would rather be left alone, the nurses persisted and won. The after effect of the bath and busyness of the day could be seen in Samuel's eyes as he was barely able to hold them open. Sleep found him. Trusting him to Susie's care, I left knowing he was in good hands.

Standing by Samuel's crib, I heard him cough. The nurse came in and felt his chest. Unwrapping her stethoscope from around her neck, she listened silently. "He sounds congested to me."

Pulling on a pair of gloves, she removed a new catheter from its packaging, fitting it snuggly on the hose attached to the suction machine. It was a fine dance to separate the tubing going to Samuel's trach, insert the catheter, suction, and reattach the tubing all without my son losing oxygen. In a flash, the nurse was done. I stared at his oxygen monitor. His oxygen levels stayed above 90 percent. An alarm didn't even go off. I was impressed. Would he do as well when we would bring him home?

Throwing her gloves and the used catheter in the trash, she turned to me. "He's needed to be suctioned several times today. I'm going to ask the doctor to order a test for RSV. We just want to rule it out. It might only be a cold."

I'd heard of RSV, respiratory syncytial virus, enough to know I didn't want my son to have it. Though common and highly contagious, for my little guy, it could become life-threatening. With no vaccine for RSV, they could only offer a medication called palivizumab as a preventative. I made a mental note to pray Samuel didn't have it.

"We'll have the test results for you tomorrow."

I nodded. I was reminded of a Bible verse:"Therefore do not worry about tomorrow, for tomorrow will worry about itself. Each day has enough trouble of its own" (Matthew 6:34, NIV). Now if I could just apply the "do not worry" to this situation.

A woman in a white doctor's coat arrived holding a clipboard. She introduced herself as an intensivist. I nodded, pretending to understand her title. Her bright eyes and wide smile put me at ease. Reading Samuel's chart, she nodded. "I'm happy with Samuel's weight gain. He's gained 50 grams today and 120 grams yesterday, totaling four kilograms."

I had to get used to the hospital using the metric system and try to calculate the total silently—1 kilogram equals 2.2 pounds so 4 kilograms equals 8.8 pounds. I was glad to hear he was gaining weight.

She interrupted my mathematical calculations. "Oh, please, thank your co-pastor for the lemon cake yesterday. We love Wright's Gourmet around here. One of the nurses mentioned buying another one. It was a big hit."

I smiled thinking about our co-pastor bringing cake. He had the gift of food. He worked part-time at one of Tampa's food institutions, Wright's Gourmet.

I nodded. "I'm so glad you enjoyed it. I'll let him know you liked it."

She put the stethoscope in her ears, leaned over, and placed the chest piece over Samuel's heart. After listening for a moment, she placed the device around her neck. "He's still a little congested, but he sounds good." She picked up the chart and read silently. I found a Kleenex to wipe Samuel's runny nose.

"We received the test back for RSV. It was negative. So it's probably just a cold we have to wait out."

Oh, thank God. Another answered prayer.

Continuing to read our son's records, she commented, "I see you have a preauthorization for a second flexie Bivona. I'm impressed. Those trachs run about one thousand dollars each."

I smiled. "I'm thankful my job is so helpful in providing Samuel with everything he needs."

"That's great."

After she completed her routine, I contemplated how amazing my employer had been. The hospital administrator told me she'd never seen a patient have such good insurance. This gave me some peace of mind. I remembered her words clearly: "Anything he needs, just let us know." *Anything* included a thousand-dollar trach. I was so thankful because it improved Samuel's breathing drastically.

Coming home, I found Ralph doing laundry and cleaning. With work and visiting the hospital, home was easily neglected. I gave my husband a grateful kiss. After I shared the events of the day from the hospital, Ralph shared his heart.

"I know I should be working getting my résumé out, but I just can't seem to push myself."

I snuggled up to him on the couch. "Honey, I know something will come up. We've got a lot on our plate right now. Just take it day by day. You've practically cleaned the whole house. Tomorrow is a new day. Get something out tomorrow. Why don't you go to bed? You'll feel better in the morning."

"You're right." He leaned over, giving me a sweet kiss. How'd I get so blessed having a wonderful husband? Not being able to fall asleep myself, I decided to write a few Christmas cards and then join my husband in bed.

Chapter 15

CHRISTMAS IN THE PICU

*C*aringbridge update: Thanks to Nurse Susie, who played different kinds of music for Samuel at night. She had a Christmas CD from Celine Dion last night. Samuel liked it, and it helped calm him down for about thirty minutes.

———

Samuel's arms reminded me of the old Michelin tire ad with tires stacked up one on another. Reaching to touch his ear, his rolls hardly stretched out. Little stubby fingers swiped back and forth, connecting with a tiny earlobe. I stood mesmerized. On a whim, I brought his little key-chain-sized stuffed toy elephant in range of his reach. An arm wildly arced, connecting with the toy as he grabbed at the snout. I laughed at the sight. Though we were in the hospital surrounded by machines and hoses, it all faded away, and it was me playing with my son.

Moments like this made the rest of the world melt away. I got to be a mother. Having to spend only visiting hours with Samuel made me feel more like a visitor than a mommy. Last night, I updated the Caringbridge website and signed the post, "Love, Evelyn, Samuel's mommy." Typing the word *mommy* reminds me of the role I play. With nurses, doctors, and staff caring for our little guy and having to leave him in the hospital at night, I didn't experience the weight of being a mother. As a first-time mom, I didn't even know what being a mother looks like. Maybe one day I'd feel like a mom.

A tiny sneeze shook his little body. I grabbed a tissue and wiped his button nose. Soon he'd get another round of immunizations. Would he get sick from the shots? He hadn't before, but there was always a chance of it, I was told. At least his weight was 8.8 pounds. If the manufacturer of the LTV ventilator was right, Samuel needed to be 11 pounds to tolerate their ventilator. If true, maybe all these trials to put him on the LTV were futile. Thankful for the break from the ventilator trials, I trusted God's timing is perfect. Maybe he would gain weight in time.

A nurse opened the door and leaned in the room as we sat beside Samuel. "We have some extra meals here. Would like to have dinner?"

I looked at Ralph. Did he want to eat here for his birthday? Before I answered, he responded, "Sure, we'll take them off your hands."

"Great. I'll be right back." The nurse closed the door.

"Are you sure you want to eat hospital food for your birthday?"

"I don't mind. It'll save us some money. We can go out for dessert later."

"But it's your birthday."

"Here we are." The nurse brought two trays, setting them on a side table. "Enjoy."

Placing the tray on my lap, we held hands and bowed our heads to pray. After saying amen, I opened the cover. Meatloaf and potatoes filled the plate. Beef is one of Ralph's favorite foods, though a big juicy steak is more in line with his tastes. He dug into the meatloaf, enjoying each bite.

"Happy birthday, my love."

"I won't be there to help when you have to do this at home." The nurse crossed his arms as he watched me attempt to change Samuel's tracheostomy tube. Some empathy would be nice, though I knew his words were true. There was comfort in knowing trained professionals were surrounding my son twenty-four hours a day. In an effort to prepare me for Samuel's homecoming, I was attempting to change the trach without the help of a nurse. I ignored the nurse's comment and gently wobbled the firm plastic tubing back and forth, hoping to slide it in into Samuel's neck through the hole surgery provided. There was black lettering on the flange stating it was a 4.5-millimeter Shiley trach.

I've got to get this in. I wanted to prove to the nurse and myself I was capable to do it. Yet I knew Samuel could only be without his trach for seconds. Realizing I must admit defeat for the sake of my son taking his next breath, I handed the trach to the nurse. Reaching across the crib with rubber-gloved hands, he accepted the breathing apparatus. Leaning over, he used his large forefinger and thumb to open the tracheostomy hole and slide the trach back in place. He made it look easy. Why couldn't I get it in?

The nurse turned to me. "If you were at home alone, you would have had to succeed. Your son's life depends on it."

My mouth dropped open at the suggestion. Though true, I'd hoped he could approach me more tactfully. Perhaps this was his attempt at tough love. This was only my first try.

I wanted to be prepared for Samuel coming home, but days like this made it seem so far away. Not only could I not put his trach in, but today's reports came back showing a bacterial virus in my son's lungs. A normal child could weather such an event, though being uncomfortable, without any serious side effects. Having a lung issue to begin with, so many things could go wrong. He had also been having desaturations and bradycardia. The staff was going to give him an antibiotic shot in his leg to counter any issues of the virus.

Samuel's hospital door creaked open. Ralph's parents walked in with big grins and a small four-foot Christmas tree.

"We come bearing gifts," Ralph's dad, Carl, said. As I gave Peggy a hug, Ralph took the artificial tree from his dad, looking around the medium-sized hospital room for the perfect spot. He placed it in the corner by the light of the window then moved it by the door and by the crib. Ralph lowered the tree by the end of the crib. "Mm, I think this might be too big for this room."

Carl waved an arm in the air. "No trouble. We can take it back. Just had it in the garage and want to offer it up for you to use."

"Thanks, Dad. I know the room needs some Christmas cheer. We'll see what we can find."

Peggy asked, "How's Samuel doing?"

Reaching out for a tissue, I used it to wipe Samuel's nose. "He's got a cold right now."

She nodded. "How are you kids holding up?"

I thought it was cute she called Ralph and I "kids." "I'm pretty busy between work and coming here. I'll be happier when he's over this cold, though."

"Well, I think you kids are doing great."

I smiled. "Thanks, Mom."

We chatted for a few more minutes before my in-laws headed out. It was so sweet of them to come and visit us. Driving home, I remembered the nurse telling us that they came to visit just the other day when we weren't here. Their concern was touching.

Sitting down at my computer, I checked for comments on Samuel's website, Caringbridge.org. Jeff Bowers, a friend from church, posted a poem:

> I thought of a poem I had read a while ago, and it made me think of you, Samuel. It was written by an old-timer named Bill Blake.
>
> Little Lamb who made thee

Dost thou know who made thee
Gave thee life and bid thee feed
By the stream and o'er the mead;
Gave thee clothing of delight,
Softest clothing wooly bright;
Gave thee such a tender voice,
Making all the vales rejoice!
Little Lamb who made thee
Dost thou know who made thee

Little Lamb I'll tell thee,
Little Lamb I'll tell thee!
He is called by thy name,
For he calls himself a Lamb:
He is meek and he is mild,
He became a little child:
I a child and thou a lamb,
We are called by his name.
Little Lamb God bless thee
Little Lamb God bless thee

You are called by His name, Baby Samuel.

A sweet encouragement to remind us God made our son. Though he lay in a hospital bed and was kept alive by machines, hoses, and wires, Samuel was called by His name.

Ralph shook my shoulder, attempting to rouse me from my slumber. "Evelyn, wake up."

"Mm, what?"

"You have to get up."

"Why are you trying to get me up?"

"It's Monday. You have to go to work."

109

Now he had my attention. I bolted upright and threw the covers off. "I need to go."

"What day did you think it was?"

I slid off the bed. "Sunday."

"Well, it's not. Wake up, sleepyhead." Easy for him to say; he was a morning person. Mumbling, I contemplated how I could have forgotten it was Monday.

"All right, I'm up."

Going into my walk-in closet, I forced my eyes open to pick out my clothes for the day. I selected a deep-brown dress with a pleated skirt and beige polka dots throughout. I jumped in the shower, using the time to pray.

"Dear Lord, I plead the blood of Jesus over Samuel. I give him into your care, and I ask that you plant your hedge of protection around him as you always do and keep him safe and in the center of your will. Help him to be the happy little man of God you called him to be. And to have a blessed day. And too Lord, please give Samuel a good nurse to take care of him. Amen."

Getting out of the shower, I dressed hurriedly. Ralph drove me to the hospital. I rushed to Samuel's side, stroking his soft blond hair and placing a kiss on his cheek before leaving again. Ralph hurried to get me to work, just managing to get me there on time.

We agreed to meet for lunch and Ralph went back to the hospital to be with Samuel. Trying to focus on work, I kept checking the time to see if it was 11:30a.m. yet. As the time approached, I cleared the papers covering my desk, grabbed my purse, hit the Out to Lunch button on my phone, and scurried to the elevator, thankful none of my representatives needed a last-minute rush to be completed.

Ralph meets me with a smile as I hop in the passenger seat, lean over offer a quick kiss. As he pulled out of the parking lot, I peppered him with questions.

"So how did it go this morning?"

"I spent most of the time trying to figure out how to bring Samuel home with the SERVO-i. I called Sunny Home Health Nursing and spoke to Leslie." Ralph turned the car north on Dale Mabry. "And you won't believe it. She knows Samuel."

"How?"

"She worked in the PICU and remembers Samuel. She is more of a can-do person. Her company doesn't carry the SERVO-i, but she wants to find out if they can get one."

Ralph turned onto Martin Luther King Jr. Boulevard toward the hospital. "That would be great. Then we could bring Samuel home now."

Ralph nodded. "She wants me to give her Samuel's current settings on the ventilator. In the meantime, she's going to check with her supervisor to see if they can rent a SERVO-i."

"That would be great." I reached over and rubbed Ralph's shoulder. "Good job thinking outside the box."

Stopping at the red light, he turned to me, offering me a cheesy grin as a way of acknowledging my praise. "We'll see what she finds out."

Turning into the parking lot, he pulled the Jeep into the first available spot. "Oh, I almost forgot to tell you. Guess who was Samuel's nurse this morning?"

"Who?"

"Stella. It makes a difference when you pray for a nurse who loves Samuel."

I smiled. "So it does."

We took a few minutes to devour our leftovers in the car and then visit Samuel. Stella was still on and gave me an update saying our little guy was having a good day. He was responding well to the antibiotic for his cold. A few minutes had passed, and I noticed it was time to go back to work. With a promise to Stella I'd be back after work, Ralph drove me back to work.

The short hours before I got off work go quickly. Ralph picked me up at 3:30p.m. with leftover stew in the back for dinner. After another good update from Stella, we decided to put Samuel in the bouncer. His questioning face made me laugh. Turning on the massager mode, he smiled. Ah, something he liked. Ten minutes into it, he made grunting sounds, letting us know he was ready for the crib. I held his hoses and followed as Ralph lifted him up and transferred him to the crib. Soon he was happily asleep, making me feel comfortable enough to go home.

Reflecting on the day, I realized it was a good one. No trauma or distress, just a happy son and a happy husband. Now if we could bring Samuel home, life would be perfect.

Leaning over the poster lying on the floor in the living room, I assessed my handiwork. In large freehand, I'd written Merry Christmas to Samuel's Helpers in black marker. I was pleased how it stood out on the red background. Several magazines were scattered around the poster, all with large holes. I picked up one of the cutouts of a picture with a red ornament hanging on a tree and glued the back of it. Placing it in the lower left-hand corner of the poster, I pressed and held it, waiting for the stickiness of the white paste to hold. I secured several more cutouts, adding a red crocheted Christmas bell and two Christmas cards. There, all done.

Ralph took one step down into the living room, peering over my shoulder. "Looks good."

I beamed. "You like it?"

"Very nice. I think we could add some photos." He paused, forehead furrowed. "I could even make the pictures in the shape of Christmas ornaments."

"That would be great." I clasped my hands together. "I hope they love it."

"I'm sure they will. By the way, Nora came by Samuel's room today. She said the flexie Bivona trach has been ordered."

"Oh, good. I know it's important to have a backup trach, especially if the one he's using gets clogged up."

"She said she doesn't know how to bill the insurance company for the extra expense."

"Oh?"

"Something about the trach company not wanting to work with the insurance company."

My heart sunk. "Do they know this trach is the only one helping Samuel breathe comfortably?"

"I'm not sure what they know, but she said she'd tell me if it doesn't go through. We don't have one thousand dollars to pay for it."

"We'll have to pray about it tonight."

He nodded. "I agree. I'm going to see what pictures I can find." As I heard his footsteps fall on the tile, taking him to the office, I closed my eyes. "Lord, please work this out as only You can. Amen."

"Santa, why don't you sit here?" The nurse pointed to the purple rocking chair next to the crib. The tall man with the kind eyes smiled under his fake white beard.

"No problem."

As he took his seat, I wondered how he was going to hold my fragile son. Did he have experience holding babies attached with wires and tubes? I could ask or trust the hospital had a Santa who knew what he was doing. I tilted my head and searched Ralph's face. He read my face perfectly and nodded, indicating he thought it was okay. Not wanting to make a fuss, I remained quiet. The nurse gently lifted Samuel from the crib with hoses under one arm and a G-tube tucked between her shoulder and her neck.

"Santa, hold your hand right here. There, that's good." She turned to me, taking the G-tube from the security of her neck. "Mom, can you hold this?"

"Sure." I took the G-tube in my hand. Not wanting to get it in the picture, I turned to Ralph. "Can you help me?"

He nodded. Grabbing a rubber band, he secured one end around the opening of the G-tube and attached the other end to Samuel's elephant toy.

Passing me the elephant, he said, "Here."

Taking the toy, I placed my hand on the high back of the chair. With my other hand, I held the tubing on the other side of Santa's arm. I looked down seeing Samuel lying snug in the crook of Santa's arm, with his hands holding tiny feet. Samuel was not smiling or frowning. It was as if he was deciding whether to be happy or sad. I heard the shutter sound of the camera and turned to see Ralph and the hospital photographer snapping pictures. There, now we had captured our son's first visit with Santa.

I smiled at Santa and looked to the nurse to help put our son back in bed before anything happened. She gently lifted him from Santa's arm and slipped the tubing under her arm, and I followed her, holding the G-tube to the crib.

Snug in his crib, I let out a sigh of relief. Nothing happened. Santa didn't drop Samuel. He didn't seem nervous holding him.

I turned to Santa. "Thank you for holding him."

"Glad to do it."

The man taking the photos smiled. "We'll have your photos ready soon. We'll bring them back to you here."

"Great. Thank you."

My mother whispered to me, "Can I hold him too?"

How could I say no since it went well with Santa? I was just going to have to trust everything would be okay.

"Sure, Mama."

The nurse placed Samuel in her arms, being sure the hoses weren't pulling on his trach. Mama looked down at Samuel snug in her arms. He was looking full into her face. I wondered what he was thinking. "Who is this holding me now?" Silence surrounded us until he wiggled back and forth. Time to get him back in the crib.

Ralph whispered to me asking if I wanted to go home with him as he took my parents back to the house. I declined, wanting to spend more time with Samuel.

Spending a few hours with Samuel gave me some alone time. Soon Ralph came back in time for my brother, his wife, and their two daughters to arrive. Visiting from Dallas, Texas, they were vacationing in Orlando.

At one point, we all held hands and bowed our heads as my brother and my sister-in-law prayed over Samuel. It is a holy, tender moment.

Taking a quiet moment, I updated Samuel's website on Caringbridge:

MERRY CHRISTMAS TO ALL from Samuel!

Samuel got to meet his Uncle Peter, Aunt Carol and cousins, Jordan & Alexandra today. Samuel was quite alert and awake for his visitors. We opened one gift today for Samuel a baby Einstein book and a cute Polo outfit that we look forward to him growing into.

Samuel gained weight again (Praise God) . . . 4.3 kilos, just under 9 1/2 pounds. Please pray specifically that he will get to 11 pounds soon for home vent trials to have the best success rate. They also lowered his oxygen to 30% from 35% which is good. We breathe 21% oxygen so this is an improvement.

In case you are wondering which Christmas card Samuel liked the best from those we showed him last weekend . . . it is from Jeff. It is a beautiful red color and in case you were wondering what Samuel was reading, it says:

BELIEVE IN MIRACLES:

THE VIRGIN BIRTH . . . "Behold, a virgin shall be with child . . . and they shall call His name Emmanuel.. God with us" Matthew 1:23.

THE RESURRECTION . . . "Ye seek Jesus of Nazareth, which was crucified: He is risen . . ." Mark 16:6

THE SOON RETURN . . . "I will come again, and receive you unto Myself; that where I am, there ye may be also." John 14:3

So, like the card says, we believe in miracles and Samuel is a beautiful miracle that we are thankful to God for. May your Christmas be filled with all the wonder of His birth. Happy Birthday, Jesus from Samuel and Samuel's Mommy & Daddy.

———w———

Arriving at the hospital, I found a satchel attached to the door handle of Samuel's room. The drawstring was tightly closed. I opened the door and entered the room without disturbing the bag.

Ralph asked, "What's in the bag?"

I shrugged. "I don't know."

The nurse heard our conversation and explained the bag was for Samuel. It was filled with toys. Each child on the floor received gifts. I took the bag off the handle and placed it next to the crib. Despite the sterile environment, a bit of home filled the room with the generosity of the gifts. The children of the hospital were not forgotten.

Pulling the string open, I pulled out the unwrapped gifts, showing each one to Samuel to see if he was interested. I smiled thinking of the generosity and kindness of strangers to be sure a child would have a small piece of Christmas when they are away from home and not feeling well.

I looked at the two strings of lights twinkling in the room. The decoration brought a tiny piece of home here too.

Chapter 16

HAPPY NEW YEAR, THE HOUSE IS ON FIRE!

Silencing my alarm next to my bed, I rolled over, wanting to snuggle deeper into the sheets. Reality slowly dawned as I realized I had to go to work today. For many people, the day after Christmas is time to spend with family, so I suspected the traffic would be light. I enjoyed seeing Samuel doing well after Christmas dinner last night, but today I was going to have to wait to visit him until after lunch.

As expected, traffic was light. Ralph dropped me off at work, arriving fifteen minutes early. I could have used the extra time to see Samuel, but I didn't want to be late for work either. Settling in at my desk, I distracted myself with paperwork. My only comfort was in knowing Ralph was going directly to the hospital.

After a few projects, I checked the time on my computer, delighted to meet Ralph for lunch. My fast-paced job helped the time melt away, and I was thankful. Just as I opened the massive glass double doors that exited to the parking lot, Ralph pulled up to the curb.

Hoping in, I moved a takeout bag from the passenger seat and slide in.

"I thought you'd like a Subway sandwich."

"Sounds good to me. Why don't we go to the park and eat there?"

Ralph drove the Pontiac to a park just north of the Raymond

James Stadium. Finding a picnic table under the shade of a tree, we prayed for our meal and began to enjoy it.

Hearing a bird singing nearby added to the peaceful environment. I tilted my head. "How was Samuel doing this morning?"

"Good. I held him in my lap for a couple of hours."

I smiled, warmed by the thought of my tall, six-foot husband cradling our little baby on his lap.

"Did he like it?"

"I think so." He grinned. "Dr. Stevens also came by to talk."

"Oh?" I braced myself.

"He said Samuel isn't ready for the home ventilator. He thinks Samuel should weigh 5.0 or 6.0 kilograms before he can go home."

I put my sandwich down. "How many pounds is 5.0 kilograms?"

"Well, that would be 2.2 pounds for every kilogram, so that's 11.0 pounds."

"He's 9.5 pounds now, so he doesn't have to gain much more."

The bird fell silent as a breeze swished the branch of the tree limb above us. I wished I could spend all day here. It was so peaceful. The report from the doctors, not so much.

A grin came across his handsome features. "I do have some good news."

He paused as I waited to hear something positive.

"Samuel gained weight. He made it to ten pounds. The nurse weighed him this morning."

"Praise God. Now he just needs to gain one more pound."

I noticed we were almost home and decided to call the hospital. Would the nurse think I was silly for calling so soon after leaving? Not letting my fear win, I dialed anyway.

Victoria answered the phone. "Hi, Victoria, I am just calling to check on Samuel. How is he doing?"

"Hi, Mom." Pause. "Um, I just left your son's room. He's okay right now, but his oxygen dropped down to eighteen."

I gasped. A normal oxygen rate is 100 percent. My brain couldn't comprehend 18 percent.

"Is he okay now? Should we come back to the hospital?"

Ralph could tell something was wrong, but he kept driving north toward home. I clutched the phone, hoping to squeeze every bit of information out of the nurse.

"Oh, no, Mom. No need to come back. He's fine now."

Breathlessly I asked, "Why did this happen?"

She responded quickly, "Oh, this is nothing new. This happens all the time." This was news to me. Hearing my pause, she added, "There is a lot you don't know."

Ralph pulled off Dale Mabry onto to North Dale Boulevard. Just a few more blocks before we were home.

I heard the nurse speaking. "Mom, he is fine now. Don't worry about it. I've got to go. My other patient's alarm is ringing."

"Uh, okay. Bye." *Click.*

I shook my head. What just happened? Should we go back to the hospital? I finished sharing with Ralph what the nurse told me as he pulled into our drive. We decided to stay home since he was doing fine and there was nothing we could do at this point.

In the morning, I told Dr. Thomlinson about Samuel's episode last night.

"Did you hear about Samuel's oxygen dropping to eighteen?"

Crossing his arms, he responded, "Yes, I know. He had a plug in his trach. Changing his trach will fix the problem. You and your husband need to be comfortable with changing the trach."

Feeling a bit like a scolded schoolgirl, I nodded. "I know. We need to get practice."

"You do that. I'm off to do rounds. Have a good morning."

Meeting Ralph at the park for lunch, I got the latest update.

Opening his sandwich wrapping, Ralph paused. "Dr. Thomlinson came to see me."

"Oh, he talked to me on my way out of the hospital this morning. He told me Samuel had a plug and strongly suggested we learn how to change Samuel's trach."

"Did he tell you what happened last night?"

I shook my head. "No."

"Mm, well, Samuel did have a plug, which caused his oxygen level and heart rate to drop. The nurse was trying to remove Samuel's plug by deep suctioning his nose. He hates it. He got so mad he held his breath and turned blue. That's why his oxygen dropped to eighteen."

I imagined the color draining from Samuel's face with his eyes squeezed shut in anger. I cringed. "I can't believe he got so mad. Hopefully the nurses know not to deep suction him."

"They may have to do it again. It may be the only way to get a plug out."

I shook my head. "Then I guess we'll pray it doesn't happen again."

Ralph nodded. "That we can do."

Samuel had been fussy, so they gave him a mucus test. I was happy to get the results, but my heart sank—he had a cold. A cold for Samuel could be serious, causing more mucus plugs to block the trach tube, potentially not allowing him to breathe. Without a clear breathing passageway, well, I didn't want to think about what would happen.

After we arrived from dinner, Samuel was awake, and though he had a runny nose, he was not fussy. Ralph read a book as I stood over my son, wiping his nose and trying to get him to reach out for his toy elephant.

We turned on the TV hearing the familiar voice of Dick Clark in the background as we put on silly hats and took pictures to commemorate the event. Just before midnight, we turned up the volume on the TV as several nurses entered our room with a bottle of bubbly apple cider to celebrate with us. The hospital room seemed like home for a moment as their act of kindness to spend this moment with our little family touched my heart. The seconds slipped away as the ball dropped, making way for 2006. What lay ahead, I didn't know, but I knew we were not alone in the journey. God had been faithful to bring my son into the world, defying the odds, proving and strengthening our faith. There was only one way to face tomorrow: with faith and lots of prayer. So after celebrating, we went home and looked at pictures from the last few months, marveling at what God had done.

Since work released everyone early on New Year's Day, I arrived at the hospital early. Ralph joined me at about 5:30p.m. and then went to forage for dinner. Shortly after he left, I got a phone call.

"Hi, honey," Ralph said.

"Hi."

"Are you sitting down?"

"Yes, I am rocking Samuel."

"I just got a phone call from someone who knows Deana." Deana is my sister-in-law. "She called to tell me that our house is on fire. I am going to go over and see what is going on."

"What do you mean our house is on fire?"

"Right now that is all I know."

I could feel my heart pounding as my mind tried to comprehend this news.

"This can't be happening."

"Don't get upset. Everything is going to be all right. We are going to be okay." Ralph's calming voice gave me assurance even though I didn't know how bad the fire damaged the house. I struggled to believe his words.

"I am on my way to the house right now. I will call you as soon as I know something."

"Okay, I will be here." Where else was I going to go? My first thought was to stay calm because I didn't want Samuel to get upset. I overheard a nurse say she couldn't believe how calm I was finding out my house was on fire. *I am trying to keep Samuel calm*, I thought.

When I was sure Samuel was not picking up on my stress, I put him back in the crib. Then I waited and paced the hospital room, wanting the phone to ring.

After about an hour, Ralph called. He explained the fire chief called him on the way to the house and told him not to speed. The damage was major, but it was not structural. When Ralph arrived, the road was blocked by six fire trucks, one ambulance, and another fire station vehicle. He had to park six houses away. The fire department broke the sliding glass door on the patio and several windows, but the fire burned itself out before they arrived. An investigator on hand ruled the fire accidental and suspected that the house caught fire from either a reignited candle or from a string of lights on the fake fichus tree in the dining room.

"I'll be there in a few minutes so you can see what happened."

After picking me up from the hospital, Ralph drove me home. Walking to the front door, I noticed Samuel's room had a broken window. Ralph opened the door to a sea of black. Charcoal sediment covered the floor in the foyer. Stepping into the dining room, the table was covered with white ash. The grapefruit we picked still sat on the table covered in soot. In the living room sat our couch turned on its side, exposing a web of wires where fabric once covered. The bookshelf, once brown wood, now appeared a sooty mess; however, the books were not burned. All our wedding photos were intact, a miracle. The binding fell apart, but the pictures were safe, tucked under the plastic. The dining room table held a wooden box with assorted wedding pictures inside. On top of the box lay a telephone handset, which completely melted. I held my breath and opened the box. Inside lay our wedding photos untouched by smoke. They were in perfect condition. Another miracle! The kitchen covered in black residue needed to be gutted.

We walked to Samuel's room and opened the door. Since the door was closed during the fire, only a little soot came through the air-conditioning vent. The beautiful mural of a seascape my sweet niece painted remained untouched. The office also wasn't damaged. In the bedroom and bathrooms, smoke seeped into the walls, leaving black streaks everywhere. Another miracle—the flames never reached the rafters. The fire died for lack of oxygen. All told, the only livable rooms were the garage, Samuel's bedroom, and the office. Every other part of the house received massive fire and smoke damage, requiring complete renovation. I could not believe this happened to our home.

Ralph's parents let us share their home, where a pullout couch awaited our arrival. Ralph's brother, also helped by taking our frightened cat, Henry, to his house. Amazingly, our feline made it out the kitty door onto the back patio, where firefighters found him.

I called off work, too upset to focus. Ralph and I met with a restoration company contracted to complete the renovations. They asked me to pick two weeks of clothes from my closet. The rest would be cleaned on a rush basis. Not only did I have a child in the PICU, but I had ten minutes to pick clothes to wear for two weeks. It seemed so surreal. I wanted to sit in the closet and cry. Instead, I placed a few clothes into a black garbage bag. With my chore done, I handed the clothes to the professionals to be cleaned.

Pushing my frustration aside, we painstakingly cataloged a list of lost items for the insurance company. Item by item we listed what was destroyed and would need to be replaced. Bookcase. Photo album covers. Couch. Stereo system. Television. The list grew and grew.

The next day we went to the house again to catalog and work with the cleaning crew. A dilemma strained within me. I wanted to be with Samuel but needed to get our house in order. I talked to the insurance company, and they offered us a hotel. I explained a hotel worked for the short run, but we needed something bigger because we were expecting our son home from the hospital soon.

We needed space for a ventilator, oxygen tanks, a crib, among other things. I could not even begin to envision all the equipment fitting into a standard hotel room. The insurance company agreed to get us into a rental home. I added house hunting to the growing list of to-dos in an already-arduous schedule.

Seeing a For Rent sign, Ralph slowed the car. After looking at several other rental options, this one looked promising, only a few blocks from our home. As I jotted down the phone number, a medium-built man with sandy-brown hair came out of the house waving to us.

"Honey, why don't we ask him about the house?"

Ralph shrugged and rolled down with window. The man took his mail from the mailbox and stepped closer to our car.

"You looking for a place to rent?"

I let Ralph talk. "Actually, we are. We had a house fire and need to rent while we wait for the renovations."

The man scratched his chin. "I heard about a house fire just a couple of blocks over. Was that you?"

New travels fast. I imagined a pillar of smoke filling the sky made many people notice as they came home from work. Still, I winced having to admit it was indeed our home. Ralph must have felt the same way as he cleared his throat.

"Yes, that was our house. It could have been worse. The structure wasn't damaged, smoke damage mostly."

Placing the mail under his arm with one hand and pointing to his house with other, he responded, "I'd be happy to help you out. Why don't you come inside and take a look?"

Happy we could see the house right away without an appointment, we followed him as he explained he was an orthodontist and a realtor. A friend of his owned the house, and he was listing it for rent.

Entering the two-story home, going past a sitting room flooded with natural light from the windows, we stepped into the entrance seeing a kitchen on our left and a sunken-in living room to our right. Standing at the railing separating the two areas, I contemplated how to situate Samuel and all his equipment. Another plus, I had a clear view of the living room from the kitchen. A half bath separated the kitchen and the front sitting room.

A quick tour of the expansive back porch overlooking a pond and viewing the upstairs bedrooms brought us to the front door again. By the time we got back in the car, the realtor offered us a month-to-month lease including use of the furniture and adding in the cost of utilities.

What a godsend. If only the insurance company would agree, this would be a great short-term solution. I left a message for my home insurance agent, praying they'd agree to the terms offered.

By the end of the day, the insurance company agreed to a hotel and the short-term monthly rental. One step closer to bringing Samuel home. Not his actual home, but not a hotel either. What a blessing God answered our prayers for help.

Checking into a local hotel, we found a lovely room with a view of Tampa Bay to greet us. Grateful to give my in-laws their couch back, we unpacked, settling in for the night. Grabbing a tissue, I wondered if my sniffles were from the soot at the house or something else. Thanks to several people from church doing inventory, I stayed away from the house. I contributed by bringing Subway sandwiches.

By morning, I had no doubt about my sniffles. Barely able to raise myself from the bed, I called in sick. Sleeping in did wonders, but I was still not myself. Revived, I meet with Ralph for lunch and felt well enough going to the office for a few hours. Once at the hospital, I put on a gown, gloves, and a mask as a precaution. As the nurse laid Samuel in my arms, I asked how he was doing, feeling awkward speaking into a mask.

"His oxygen level is in the nineties. We'd like to see it higher, in the mid- to high-nineties range. We're running some tests right now, but we think it's viral rather than bacterial."

"Will you give him anything to help?"

"Not if it's viral. The cold has to run its course."

I nodded. Hopefully, mine would go away soon. I used my gloved hand to be sure my mask covered my mouth. I focused on Samuel, who was content, not fussing at all.

While Ralph was talking to his dad on the phone, I continued to enjoy this precious moment. I didn't think they'd be sending Samuel home with a cold. I was happy we had someplace to bring him home to. Ralph said the contractor believed our home renovation would take six months. Sounded like a long time to me.

Not wanting to contribute to Samuel's cold, I gently placed him back in the crib. I didn't want to leave but knew it was for the best.

Ralph was in the big purple chair when I arrived at the hospital during lunch break. Offering him a quick kiss, I walked to Samuel's crib.

"How is he doing?"

Ralph got up and stood next to me. "I saw Dr. Lyon during rounds this morning and was told he didn't have a good morning. Samuel was happy when I came, even giving me smiles. His nurse Taylor was shocked. She couldn't explain why he was doing so well all of a sudden."

I smiled. "Maybe he likes having his Daddy around."

He nodded. "Maybe. The test results also came back for Samuel's cold. It's neither viral or bacterial."

"Really? That's odd."

"I agree. They are going to keep a close eye on it. I hope he stays happy like this morning."

Samuel's chubby little arms were attempting to reach his chin as he cooed in the mirror. He flashed me a brilliant smile. Delighted by my son's happiness, I could go back to the office better than I felt. I was still a bit out of it, but good enough to work. Ralph eyes had dark circles under them.

"You don't look so perky."

Ralph stretched both arms over his head and yawned. "Yeah, I didn't get much sleep last night. I have a couple of errands to run but will probably go to the hotel to rest."

Giving him a side hug, I responded, "Well, you take care of yourself. I can't imagine both of us being sick. We need to be here for Samuel."

Looking at the clock, he added, "You better get going, or you'll be late for work."

Visiting the hospital for lunch had caused me to be late a couple of times. I always made up the time, but I didn't want to take advantage of my company's kindness and grace toward me.

"Oh, you're right. Going to grab something at the cafeteria and hurry back now. Bye, my love. See you after work."

Getting off at 3:00p.m., I rushed back to the hospital. Calling Ralph on the way, he told me he was taking a nap. I arrived just in time to see Stella, one of our favorite nurses.

"How is Samuel doing?"

She frowned. "He's not having his best day. Samuel's oxygen level dropped, and he turned color when I found him. I stabilized him. I'm so glad I found him. I'm not even his nurse today."

"What happened?"

She shrugged. "The best I can come up with is some mucus blocked his airway in the trach tube."

I looked behind Stella to peek through the window of his room. "How is he now?"

"He's still a little fussy. Why don't you go in? I'm on the floor if you need me, but Jeanette is his nurse this shift."

I gave her a quick hug. "Thank you so much for keeping an eye out for Samuel."

Opening the door, I rushed to Samuel's side. He was alone. His arms and legs were moving as he made a whiney noise through his throat, bypassing the trach.

I stroked his leg, leaned over, and whispered in his ear, "Mommy is here. I love you. Mommy loves you."

His hand touched my cheek. I melted.

The nurse opened Samuel's door. "Hi, Mom, I'm Jeanette. Stella told me you were here."

"Hi, Jeanette. Do you think you can help me hold Samuel? I think it might help."

"Absolutely."

After several adjustments, Samuel was snuggled in the crook of my arm with his ventilator tubes draped over my arm and secured with tape to the rocking chair.

After Jeanette left, I rocked the chair and sang "Jesus Loves Me." I lost track of time as I sang every song I knew from memory. Samuel's eyes dropped off to sleep. Oh, thank God. As gently as I could, I slipped my sleeping angel back into the crib and sneaked off to the ladies' room.

Going back to the room, Ralph arrived with a bag of takeout Chinese food in hand.

Just as we finished dinner, Samuel woke up crying. Jeanette came in and checked on Samuel and slipped out of the room. My stroking, cooing, and singing was not helping now. I looked up at Ralph, worried.

Jeanette opened the door holding a syringe in her hand. "The doctor said to give him some chloral hydrate. Hopefully it will help."

She opened the side port of the G-tube, inserted the syringe, and delivered the medicine. From previous experience, I knew it would take about twenty minutes for the medicine to start helping. I checked the clock.

Ralph and I were silent as we waited for the minutes to tick away. He was sitting in the rocking chair as I stood by the crib, holding Samuel's hand. Samuel's cries ricocheted through my body like a lightning bolt. I closed my eyes, praying for the medicine to work. To my utter relief, the medicine started working, and though he was not asleep, he'd stopped crying.

I looked up at Ralph. Relief etched on his face. He got up and stood next to me, placing an arm on my shoulder. We exchanged no words. We both stared at our son, thankful for the quiet in the room. The whooshing of the ventilator was almost soothing.

Ralph broke the silence. "I think we should let our little guy get some rest. You need it too. It's already 10:00p.m."

I leaned my head on his shoulder. He leaned over, placing a kiss on my forehead.

"I know you're right. I'm a bit worn-out over this episode. Let's go back to the hotel."

I leaned over and kissed Samuel's forehead. He gave me a half smile as if he was saying, "I'm okay now, Mommy. You can go home." I tucked his smile in my heart and took Ralph's hand as we left the hospital room.

Our hotel bedroom window was next to an outdoor hallway overlooking the parking lot. The drapes were closed, but I could still hear footsteps outside. Who could be up at this time of the morning? Some early riser either eager to get started on a day of exploring or, like me, needing to get to work on time. I looked over at Ralph still sleeping and decided not to wake him up. Usually he was an early riser, but this cold had him down.

By midmorning, my cell phone rang.

"Hi, my love. I'm about to go into the elevator, so if you lose me, I'll call you back. I heard you leave this morning, and I slept for another couple of hours. That helped. I just arrived at the hospital about an hour ago."

"I'm glad you're there. Are you feeling better?"

"A little, but Samuel isn't doing so good."

"What's going on?"

"I talked to Samuel's night nurse, Thomas. He said Samuel's heart rate dropped down to twenty beats per minute. He had to do chest compressions on Samuel to bring his heart rate back up."

I closed my eyes, imagining Thomas pushing on my son's tiny chest. I couldn't picture it. It's too hard. I open my eyes and realize Ralph is still talking.

"Thomas was able to bring Samuel's heart rate back up, but then Stella came on this morning, and his heart rate again dropped, this time to fifty beats per minute, and his oxygen level dropped to 20 percent."

I squeezed my eyes close remembering Samuel's oxygen level was determined by a blood oxygen saturation reading indicating the percentage of hemoglobin molecules in the arterial blood. Had we still had the DNR in place, Samuel would not have been revived. Little did I know, Dr. Lyon had asked Ralph to reinstate the DNR just nine days ago. Claiming Ralph was the more rational one, he chose to discuss the issue with my husband. Since we had our house fire that day, Ralph decided not to overload me.

Letting out a deep breath, I asked, "How's he doing now?"

"I held him, but that didn't calm him down. They gave him some Tylenol, which helped."

For the hospital to give him Tylenol, he must have been fussy. They didn't give him Tylenol when he had a cold, hoping his little body would fight the infection on its own.

Ralph interrupted my thoughts. "I am sure the doctors will be by any minute now giving me a doom-and-gloom scenario because of these episodes."

I sputtered, "Isn't he better now, though?"

"Yes, but you know how the doctors can be."

"Yes, I know." I checked my watch. "Honey, I've got to go. My break is over. Will you stay there until I get there on my lunch break?"

"I'll wait for you."

"Good. And call me if something changes. I can always tell my boss I have to go."

"Will do. See you soon."

I braced myself for the blast of cold air as I reentered the glass office building. Trying to absorb what happened, I couldn't comprehend losing Samuel. I prayed for God to protect him.

Days merged from one into another as a predictable routine ensued. We'd get up, go to work, visit Samuel, rest at the hotel, and then awake to start another day. The main concern confronting us was getting Samuel to overcome this cold, which was causing havoc with his respiratory system.

The nurse told me he had a rough night, experiencing several episodes where his oxygen and heart rate dropped three times. His heart rate dropped as low as thirty-six beats per minute.

The good news was he recovered each time. This stubborn cold, his third since being in the hospital, was not letting go. I couldn't help wonder if he was picking these colds up in the hospital. Would he be better at home? The nurse said they were treating this cold with double antibiotics in an effort to knock it out. I could only pray it would work.

Torched bookshelf - Photographs untouched

A Sea Of Black surrounding Florida Grapefruits.

Chapter 17

A SCARE AND A
SURPRISE VISITOR

*W*e decided to go to the mall to get some errands done. Calling the hospital for an update, I was happy Stella answered the call and was on duty with Samuel. She checked his numbers, assuring me he was having a great day.

I told Ralph the good news, and we drove the twenty-minute drive to the hospital. Arriving in the PICU, we were surprised when Stella asked to talk to us privately. When I noticed the normally jovial Stella wasn't smiling, I was concerned. I turned, looking at Samuel's room.

"He's doing fine. There's a room right around the corner here."

Turning to Ralph, I shrugged my shoulders and followed Stella. We entered an empty meeting room.

"First off, I say this not to worry you, but I thought you should know."

Oh, no. Is Samuel all right? But didn't she just tell us he's all right?

Ralph slipped his hand in mine. Stella had our full attention.

Stella, still standing, held her hands together. Her face was pale. "When you called, I checked Samuel's monitors, and his numbers were great. I hung up the phone after talking to you and checked his numbers again. His oxygen saturations were fine, but his heart rate dropped really low."

She paused. I was sure I didn't want to hear what she was going

133

to say next, but I also knew I needed to know. Noting our silence, she continued. "So I grabbed the Ambu bag and disconnected the ventilator tubing. His heart stopped beating for a three-second interval."

She took a breath while wiping away a tear.

I froze. Her tears made her words real. I looked around for the nearest chair. I needed to sit down. Pulling over a conference table chair, I let it hold me. Stella grabbed a tissue from the table while Ralph got another chair to sit next to me.

She apologized. "I'm sorry for my tears. It just scared me."

I was shook up but able to respond, "What happened next?"

She sniffled. "We were able to bring his heart rate back up, and now he's acting like nothing happened. He's fine now."

Ralph cleared his throat. "What can we do so this doesn't happen again?"

"I'm not sure." She paused again and looked back and forth to both of us. "He almost died."

I shook my head, wishing her words to be unspoken.

Ralph nodded. "Could reducing his feed help?"

She leaned back in her chair. "It might. We can reduce his intake from twenty-six milliliters per hour to twenty-one milliliters."

I listened to Ralph and Stella talk, trying to find an answer. Losing Samuel was unthinkable. Stella's tears made my own well up. Grabbing a tissue, I dried my eyes. Even with our favorite nurse on, Samuel had a major event. Nothing was certain. I couldn't keep my son alive, only God could.

Stella's words broke my reverie. "I think we should focus on keeping Samuel alive right now. We can cut back on his feed and wait to do the home ventilator trials."

Ralph nodded. "I agree."

Stella looked at me. "We also might need to give Samuel chloral hydrate for the next couple of days to help him through this."

I agreed. "Whatever it takes to keep him with us."

Stella held her hands over her heart. "You know I'll do whatever I can for your son. I care for him as if he were my own."

I knew her words were true. Even having this private meeting with us showed us her care and concern. I always trusted Samuel would be okay when she was on duty, but know, especially after today, she wasn't able to keep our little guy alive. I was so glad she checked his numbers again after we called. She saved his life today.

We both stood up, and I opened my arms to hug her. I whispered in her ear, "Thank you so much for being there for Samuel."

When we saw Samuel, he was smiling. This is what family feels like, together, weathering the storms of life. And with God, nothing is impossible.

Though Samuel had a good day, Dr. Peterson suggested another meeting of the nurses, staff, and doctors. The reports of Samuel's scare must have had reached his ears. Though Samuel's heart rate hadn't dropped since and his cold was gone, they believed there was still concern. Samuel, not knowing what all the fuss was about, was back to his happy disposition. His dietician was even pleased with his weight gain.

As we got ready for bed, I remembered to tell Ralph about a visitor.

"My love, I invited Robbie's mom to come visit us."

He repositioned his pillow. "That's great."

I turned off the light next to the bed thinking about meeting Jennifer Schouest. Her son, Robbie, had type 2 TD. He did not need a ventilator. He had to evacuate with his mom when Hurricane Katrina threatened her home town in Louisiana. Shortly after they were given the all clear to come home, little Robbie didn't make it. Jennifer thought it was perhaps from the toll of traveling. It would be wonderful to meet another mom who had a TD child, but sad at the same time.

Watching Ralph put together the Baby Einstein mobile warmed my heart. Being an engineer by trade, this was easy for him. Seeing him perform the fatherly function brought a smile to my lips. Slowly all the pieces fit together and began to take shape. Finding a place to attach the mobile to the metal crib frame, Ralph made a few twists, completing the task. Plugging it in and flipping a switch, the music turned on as the mobile circled above Samuel's head.

Samuel reached for the mobile, but his hands came up short. He rolled on his side as I scrambled to adjust the ventilator tubing so it was not tugging on his neck. This time, his hand barely reached the mobile. As the mobile made its decent, he swatted at it. In the middle of all the tubes, machines, and wires, my boy had found a piece of joy.

Bang. Boom. "Honey, what are you doing?"

"Packing. We have to check out today?"

How could I have forgotten? Perhaps this flu had affected my memory. The thought of rolling out of bed was more effort than I could manage. I pulled the pillow over my head, hoping to drown out the noise. I dosed off feeling bad leaving all the packing for Ralph.

Ralph's hand gently touched my shoulder. "My love, aren't you going to get up?"

Opening one eye, I considered my options. Sleeping more was at the top of my list. I couldn't think of anything else I'd rather do. Ralph sat on the side of the bed.

"I've got most everything packed. You need to pack your things, and we can go."

"Okay, give me a minute, and I'll get up."

His eyebrow rose.

Pouting my lip out, he smiled.

"Only a minute, but remember, checkout time is soon."

I closed my eyes again. This time, I couldn't sleep knowing we had to go. Getting up, I headed to the shower. The hot water helped to waken me. Now I needed a cup of tea to finish the job. The kitchenette provided a coffee pot, which I used to make tea. The steamy tea was too hot to drink, so I set it down. Still groggy, I packed my suitcase and the toiletries.

Carrying everything down the stairs, we turned our keys in. Time to pick up the rental house keys and relocate to our new temporary home, the first home Samuel would experience outside of the hospital. I wished it were our real home, but I was thankful not to be bringing him to a hotel.

After picking up our keys, we pulled up the steep driveway ready to unload the meager belongings we retrieved from the house after the fire. I was thankful the rental house was fully furnished, including a stocked kitchen.

The cool air greeted us as we opened the front door. Ralph searched for the A/C control to turn on the main unit in the large two-story home. I walked into the kitchen, which overlooked the sunken living room. This was going to work out great, being able to see Samuel while I was in the kitchen. The sink was clean, but seeing crumbs scattered around the toaster, I got to work, cleaning it up. Must be from the previous renters. After wiping down the counters, I peeked in the front living room by the entrance. Everything looked clean here; however, the curtains were closed. I banished the darkness by opening the curtains, which revealed large bay windows, allowing the sunlight to soak the area. There, that was a bit better. The dark-brown couch reminded me of furniture from the 1980's. Still, it was better than bringing Samuel to a hotel.

Turning around, I walked up the stairway holding on to the wooden bannister leading to two upstairs bedrooms and a bathroom. Entering the smaller bedroom nearest the stairway, I sat on the bed and fell back. A seam split the bed in two. I realized the mattress was two singles pushed together. I frowned. Ralph entered the bedroom.

"What's wrong?"

I sat up. "This bed is so uncomfortable. It's two mattress pushed together."

Ralph sat next to me. I moved over so he could feel the seam. He lay back and paused. "Mm, I see what you mean."

Seeing the half-open door to the master bedroom, we inspected its contents. A double bed was in the center of the room with the bathroom to the right. A large dark-brown dresser occupied much of the room along with the bed.

Ralph sat on the bed. "This isn't too bad. How about we swap the twin mattresses with this double?"

"I guess that makes sense. I'd rather be near the stairwell so we can be as close as possible to Samuel."

Ralph followed me downstairs. "The doctors said they are going to do a trial to get Samuel on the home vent today. I think one of us should be there."

I stopped in the hallway. Turning, I faced Ralph. "I agree."

"Why don't you go to church and I'll go the hospital?"

I nodded. "Sounds good."

Ralph walked to the dining room table to pick up his keys. "I'll call the hospital and ask them to hold off on the trial until I get there."

I was relieved Samuel would have Ralph's comforting presence to calm him. "Okay."

Grabbing my purse and keys, I stood on my tiptoes to offer a parting kiss. "I'll call you after church."

As I enjoyed a snack in the fellowship hall after church, Ralph entered, looking for me. I waved as he spotted me. After grabbing a cup of coffee, he made his way to my table.

Not being able to hold back my curiosity, I asked, "How'd it go?"

After taking a sip of dark coffee, he placed the Styrofoam cup down. "They didn't do the trial. No one ever came to do it. Dr. Peterson called off the test. I waited for him to come talk to me about why, but after waiting twenty minutes, I thought I'd just come to church."

What could have caused the cancellation? "How's Samuel?"

"He's doing fine."

Good news.

Our co-pastor approached our table. Tall; bushy, curly hair; and a genuine smile graced his face. He handed Ralph a Styrofoam to-go container filled with food. He must have seen Ralph come in after lunch was packed away and thought to make a plate for my hubby. Many times he brought us sandwiches to the hospital. I smiled watching the exchange. A gift of food is always welcome.

Arriving for my lunch hour, Ralph gave me the update. "He's sleeping now, but I needed to hold him most of the time. And he had to be suctioned a lot more than yesterday. I don't think it's a good day to do a trial on the home vent."

I wanted to stroke Samuel's arm but didn't want to disturb his slumber. "Doesn't sound like it."

Ralph ran his fingers through his hair. "I told Dr. Lyon we should wait another day. He agreed."

I frowned. "Samuel should rest for now and do the trial when he feels better."

"I agree." Ralph's eyes lit up. "I did talk to Susie, the respiratory therapist, about how to make the next trial more successful. She agreed to cut down on his feedings and to wait until he's asleep to switch him to the home vent."

That sounded brilliant. Maybe he wouldn't notice the switch if he was sleeping.

Ralph continued, "It makes sense to try it since he was fighting against the vent yesterday."

I nodded. "Something has to work. If we could only take the SERVO-i home, then we wouldn't need to do all these trials and take Samuel home."

Ralph gave me a hug. "I know, my love. Oh, by the way, I spoke to Nora, and she's worried about you."

My mouth dropped. "Why?"

"She thinks you're not getting enough sleep. I told her about our move and that you are getting over a cold."

I couldn't imagine when she would have noticed. It was true.

Working a 7:00a.m. to 3:00p.m. shift and coming to the hospital three times a day was taking its toll on my sleep, but still.

Ralph touched my shoulder. "I also told her you are doing fine."

I smiled. "Thank you, my love." Noticing the time on the wall clock, I noticed I had to go or I'd be late. "Honey, I've got to go. Are you going to stay?"

He nodded. "I'll stay around for a little while longer. If Samuel is okay, then I'll check on the guys renovating the house."

I offered a quick kiss. "Sound's good. See you later."

Getting into my car, the clock light on the dashboard read 4:05p.m.

Arriving at 4:30p.m., I greeted Ralph with a kiss. Getting the rundown of Samuel's day was like getting a briefing at the White House.

- He had issues with a bowel movement. Needed to be bagged.
- Ralph worried Samuel's bowel movement issue would prevent LTV trial.
- Ralph requested Samuel's feeds be cut back during the trial. Dr. Peterson agreed.

Ralph offered each point as I listened intently. Scooping Samuel up in my arms, being careful with his hoses, I gently rocked him in the big purple chair.

"Oh, and Dr. Lyon thought the trial won't be much of a success. So I asked him about plan B. I was hoping he would suggest weaning him on pressure."

"What'd he say?"

Ralph leaned back in his chair with a half grin as he scratched the back of his head. "Well, he said, 'We look at his x-rays and wonder how he can be so happy.'"

I smiled. Our baby boy was breaking the mold. On Monday, after looking at his x-rays and the severity of his inverted diaphragm, Dr. Peterson said he was not sure how he breathed at all. I didn't know either, but my son was here and very much alive.

Ralph leaned forward. "Remember when Dr. Lyon told me it's lucky Samuel can't read the textbooks?"

"Yes, and it's so true. I love watching God work."

No one had hope in this child. Yet Samuel was still on the home ventilator. The swooshing sound was much louder than the SERVO-i. The tubing delivering the breaths shook with each push. No alarms pierced the room. Samuel lay contently in my arms. I wondered what Dr. Peterson would think of this successful trial.

Ralph cleared his throat. "I told Dr. Lyon 'Full speed ahead.' He smiled and told me 'Maybe 1/10th speed ahead.'"

I laughed imagining Ralph standing his full six-foot height, hand raised in the air, saying "Full speed ahead!" while Dr. Lyon responded in his lilting South African accent and a half grin.

"So how did Samuel do when he was taken off the SERVO-i?"

Ralph smiled. "Suzette switched him while I distracted him with a book. After the switch, I put his toys within reach." Standing up to lean on the crib, Ralph continued, "They checked his blood gas at about 1:00p.m., and it was 42 percent CO_2, which is right on target."

Our son continued to surprise the doctors.

The doors to the elevator close before I could hit the down button. Six elevators, and all of them were busy. All I could think about was the bad review I received at work. Keeping up on my daily tasks while struggling to visit Samuel three times a day made an impact on my production. Being encouraged to do overtime to keep up seemed an overwhelming suggestion given my current circumstances.

Ding. Ah, now I could escape.

As I pulled out of the parking lot, I contemplated where to add a few hours to my day. If I took a half-hour lunch, I wouldn't be able to visit Samuel. I could work a half hour extra each day. Or maybe come in on Saturday. I was worn-out without overtime hours. Not coming up with a quick solution, I resolved to focus on seeing Samuel.

Ralph greeted me with a kiss as I entered Samuel's room. I heard the swoosh of the home ventilator. Sure enough, it was on and hooked up to Samuel. My mouth opened. Ralph was smiling. I knew the look on his face, the I-told-you-so look.

Going to the crib, Samuel batted his hand at the mobile as it swung around. I laughed. Yes, I'd say he was doing good.

"Your morning went better than mine."

Sitting in the chairs next to the crib, I shared the review I received at work. Maybe my husband could problem solve this issue.

Ralph took my hands in his. "My love, don't worry about it. First of all, you don't have time for overtime right now. I need you, and Samuel needs you. Don't focus on that."

I let out a sigh of relief. Everything in perspective.

After getting a surprise phone call, I reached Ralph on his cell as I pulled into the hospital parking lot.

"Hi, honey. I'm on my way to see Samuel, but you won't believe who I got a call from."

"Who?"

"Robbie's mom. She is in town and wants to come meet Samuel. Can you be at the hospital by 5:30p.m.?"

"Sure. I'm at the rental house. The cat got out again."

"Oh, great. Hope you find him, honey. See you soon."

"Okay, be there soon."

A cold wind blew as I got out of the car. Thankful for the pink sweater I picked out this morning, I took quicker strides to get indoors. I found my way to Samuel's room, glad for the warmth of the building.

I told the nurse about Samuel's visitor, Jennifer Schouest, Robbie's mom. She listened as I shared he was the only child we knew with type 2 thanatophoric dysplasia. Remarkably, he survived without a ventilator at birth, only using a nose cannula.

She nodded. I further explained the story. Shortly after Hurricane Katrina, Jennifer and her family evacuated from Louisiana to another state for safety. Upon returning, little Robbie, at nine months old, passed away.

She nodded. "That's so sad."

"Yes, it is."

As the nurse was called away, I pondered, *Will visiting Samuel bring Jennifer comfort?* I hoped so.

Jennifer, with long brown hair and a bright smile, hugged me after being buzzed into the PICU by the on-duty nurse. Ralph looked on from the entrance to Samuel's room. To meet another mom who could truly understand our circumstances was a blessing I thought I would never know. The moment must be bittersweet knowing her son, Robbie, was not here.

We entered Samuel's room just as Dr. Lyon arrived. After introducing him to Jennifer, he told us he was originally out of Louisiana and even knew the area where Jennifer was from. Small world.

Jennifer approached Samuel's crib while Dr. Lyon continued speaking to Ralph. She was silent, motionless, beholding my son. I wondered if she was remembering Robbie. Samuel continued watching his mobile, unaware of our special visitor.

Pulling out sweet pictures of her son, Robbie, she mentioned his challenges with seizures and the grueling evacuation he endured.

Dr. Lyon asked Ralph for an update.

"He's been on the home ventilator since yesterday."

Scratching his head, Dr. Lyon smiled. "Again, my crystal ball is wrong."

I chuckled, storing the doctor's words in my heart.

Dr. Lyon nodded. "I really didn't think he would be doing this well."

Not able to hold back, I asked the question I'd been wanting to hear, "When do you think Samuel can come home?"

He paused. "In about a week, but don't get too excited about his progress. There are rocky roads ahead."

That soon. The day I'd been praying for was coming, against all predictions, exceeding even Dr. Lyon's predictions. From his genuine smile, he shared in our joy.

And Jennifer was here to hear this good news. It was a good day.

Ralph wrapped his arm around my waist, pulling me to his side. Laugh lines appeared by his eyes. I beamed back at my husband, sensing we had won a victory, a battle without weapons forged by faith and prayer.

Jennifer mentioned she needed to leave since her family was waiting in the car. She pressed a ceramic hand holding a baby into my hands and gave me a smile and hug.

On the way out, I introduced Jennifer to Dr. Peterson, who asked her a few questions. She answered, gave me another hug, and left the NICU. After the doors closed, Dr. Peterson shrugged his shoulders, commenting, "Why didn't Robbie get a trach? He may be here today." I was silent.

After Jennifer's visit, I remembered Dr. Lyon's caution about rocky days, causing me to quell my mini celebration. As Ralph led me to the cafeteria for dinner, I realized we had won a battle. I would not think about what lay ahead, but instead I'd sleep well tonight knowing my son would soon be home.

The gentle motion of the rocking chair was having no effect. Samuel's silent cry unnerved me. Tears rolled down his cheeks. How could I calm him? I rocked faster and stroked his arm with my hand. Hoping my soothing voice would help, I whispered in his ear, to no avail. An alarm pierced the hospital room as his nurse rushed in and grabbed the Ambu bag.

Methodically inflating and deflating the balloon, she watched the monitor until the alarm ceased. Samuel's mouth opened wider as his eyes were shut tight. The extra oxygen kept the dusky color of his skin away but did not ease his discomfort. The nurse assured me she'd be right back with some Tylenol.

I knew how conservative the staff was about using Tylenol. With his last cold, they used it as a last resort, wanting the cold to take its course, allowing his body to fight it. Not today.

Having drawn up the correct dosage, the nurse entered with a loaded syringe. Opening the port in his G-tube tubing, she delivered the liquid acetaminophen through the tube to his stomach. I looked at the clock, checking off the twenty minutes it took to be effective.

Closing my eyes while still rocking, I prayed, silently imploring God to calm my son. A hand touched my shoulder, startling me. My husband's concerned face filled my view. He knelt down next to us, his hand stroking my arm. He touched Samuel's forehead. I saw the numbers drop on the monitor, setting off his oxygen alarm again.

Nothing we were doing was helping. The nurse once again brought up his oxygen using the Ambu bag. Finishing her task, she commented, "Let's try something stronger this time. I'll get the chloral hydrate."

Ralph nodded. This drug should calm him down. Though I didn't want to give him something so strong, there was no other choice.

Ricky, the respiratory therapist arrived. With a clipboard in one hand, he adjusted the settings on the ventilator. Ralph stood next to him, observing the changes. Ralph turned to me, eyebrows knitted, shaking his head.

The swooshing sound of the home ventilator filled the air, not having to compete with piercing alarms.

The nurse administered the drug. I prayed it would calm him down. She commented, "Maybe we should put him back on the SERVO-i."

Ralph agreed. This was a setback to bringing him home. My heart sank. We were so close to our goal. Looking at my son's discomfort, I knew it was the right thing to do.

Laying him back in the crib, Ricky switched ventilators in

seconds. Samuel's face started to relax. Was it the chloral hydrate or the ventilator breathing for him that worked? I released a pent-up sigh. The room was more peaceful with the soft sounds of the SERVO-i in the background.

Turning to Ralph, I grinned. Ralph said, "Well, at least he was on the home ventilator for two and a half days." Looking at the clock, he added, "Minus an hour."

I nodded. "I just hope this is not a major setback. We can't take the SERVO-i home."

The nurse returned to the nurses' station, leaving us alone as Samuel's eyes drooped, heavily exhausted from the effort of the day.

Ralph stepped close to me. "I saw Luke, the respiratory therapist, changing the settings on Samuel's home ventilator. I know the settings Suzette used were working. Maybe that's why Samuel had a hard time. I took a picture before Ricky changed the settings again."

Why couldn't we have Suzette as Samuel's only RT, as we requested? As long as Ralph was here during the trials, he could at least check the settings so Samuel could tolerate the trial.

I leaned into Ralph. "I wish we could get all the respiratory therapists on the same page. At least you are keeping an eye on it."

He rubbed the back of his neck. "I can't be here all the time. I'll ask when Suzette is going to be on again. Maybe she can help."

I nodded. "Wouldn't that be wonderful." Looking at the clock, it was well after 9:00p.m. Samuel's eyes were closed.

Ralph followed my gaze. "Why don't we call it a night? He's stable now."

Agreeing to go home, I buried my concern. Standing next to the crib, I offered a quick, silent prayer and then took Ralph's hand.

Arriving home, Ralph headed to the office, printing out the picture, while I changed into pajamas. He came into the bedroom with the printout in his hand raised over his head.

"I have proof here. Luke was wrong. Those settings were not the same settings Suzette set up, which we know works."

Oh my. "What are you going to do?"

Pacing the room, he waved the paper in the air. "I'll show Suzette this picture and request she be on for the next vent trial."

Slipping into bed, I pulled up the covers. "If her settings work, then I would think the hospital would want to use them so Samuel can come home."

Falling in bed next to me, Ralph continued, "You would think."

Turning off the night-light, Ralph reached out. After we prayed, he gave me a hug. I offered a kiss good-night but was too tired to offer Ralph anything more.

—⚬—

Another day, another vent trial. Thankfully, Stella was on today. I knew I shouldn't place all my trust in the nurses, but it gave me great comfort to know she loved our little guy and would do anything for him. Dr. Peterson ordered to have Samuel placed back on the home ventilator.

As the clock turned to 11:00a.m., he was taken off the SERVO-i and placed on the noisier home ventilator. Stella, Ralph, and I stood around the crib watching Samuel's stomach for any clues of belly breathing. There was no change. I looked at the monitor above his bed. The red numbers weren't flashing with a cry of an alarm to startle us.

Closing my eyes briefly, I offered God a silent prayer of thanks. Ralph turned to me, a grin beginning at the corner of his mouth. Wrapping my arm around his, I let out a sigh.

Approaching Samuel's crib, I leaned over the rail to take a close look. Waving his arm to swat at the mobile traveling in a circle above his head, he was unaware of his parents' concern. Isn't that the way it should be, a mother worrying and a child not worrying because his mother is there? I turned the churning thoughts in my mind over to God in the same way a child trusts his parent.

Stella tilted her head. "I have an idea. Why don't you two get out and enjoy your Saturday? The transfer went great, and he's happy."

I tilted my head. Ralph was nodding.

147

Stella shifted her weight. "Really, he's fine."

I nodded. "You'll call us?"

"Absolutely. Now you two go and enjoy."

I kissed Samuel on the forehead and took Ralph's outstretched hand into mine. I needed to trust God with Samuel even if we were gone for a little while. I never thought my heart could be so bound to my child. One last look over my shoulder, and in minutes we were out of the cold confines of the hospital, standing in the shining afternoon sun. The difference was stark and welcome.

"Why don't we check out cabinets for the house?"

Turning the corner to the parking garage, I calculated how far the store was from the hospital. About twenty minutes, I figured. That'd work.

"Let's try it."

Ralph raised his eyebrows and, looking like a kid, grinned from ear to ear.

"Let's go."

After Sunday night dinner, I only wanted the comfort of my bed. Not even the appeal of shopping could drag me out of the house. As I lay on the bed, I delighted in the good news of Samuel still being on the home ventilator. Next to going to church, this was the highlight of the day.

Ralph made me his family recipe of macaroni and cheese for dinner. Nothing like good comfort food to ease my cravings. And afterward we had communion together. A sweet blissful moment to calm my heart, centering me in my faith.

With a warmth in my belly, a centered faith, and a son doing well, sleep whisked me away quickly. At least in this moment, all was well.

I nervously kept my cell phone by my side. Whether I was in the break room, at the photocopier, or taking a break, I clutched the device, not wanting to miss a call.

Samuel was having an in-room operation done to take out the old G-tube and replace it with a new one. Though these procedures were routine, quick, and usually problem free, this momma heart was on high alert.

My phone rang at 10:00a.m.

I answered on the second ring. "Hello."

"Hi, my love. I knew you would want an update. The procedure finished about a half hour ago, and Samuel came through fine."

I slumped back into my chair. "Oh, thank God."

"I thought you'd be pleased. I'll stick around for a little while, but things seem to be going well enough. I'm going to get some errands done."

"Okay. I will go visit Samuel during lunch. Thanks for updating me. I was on pins and needles waiting for your call."

After finishing the call, I attempted to focus on the task at hand. I managed to complete several easier items on my to-do list before leaving for lunch.

Finding Samuel alone in his hospital room, I checked the monitors and noticed his oxygen level was hitting 100 percent. Knowing I could reduce the amount of oxygen he was receiving, I turned the dial down. Zoe, Samuel's nurse, entered the room, and saw the adjustment I made. She paused.

"You know you're not supposed to touch the equipment, right?"

I thought better of defending myself. Heat rose to my face. I couldn't imagine not being able to help Samuel if the staff wasn't here to do it. Pondering this dilemma, my phone rang. It was Kelly Sierra telling me which home health company we would be using for Samuel's nursing at home. I closed my eyes and listen to Kelly drone on about the details. I grasped the chair feeling my blood pressure rise. I didn't like being *told* which company would be selected for my son. Didn't I get a say in which company we would use? What about Sunny Home Health Nursing? How did Twin Lakes Nursing

Services get assigned to our son's case? I politely hung up with Kelly, not voicing my objections.

Knowing my lunch time was running out, I leaned over Samuel's crib and stroked his arm. Trying to block out my rising frustration, I cooed over my son.

"Hi, honey. Mommy's here. I love you."

Sweet eyes focused on the sound of my voice as a brilliant smile exploded on his face, revealing sweet dimples on each side. I threw my head back and laughed out loud. How did my son know this was what I needed right now? I leaned over and kissed his forehead.

Holding my son brought me a sweet bliss not known before becoming a mother. Yes, hoses were taped to my shirt so they didn't pull on Samuel's trach. I was surrounded by four sterile walls and a myriad of machines and monitors. The setting faded away as the close to eleven pounds of softness lay sweetly against my chest. His monitors stayed silent as if my body was calming him, providing the long ancient touch of a mother's love. This was motherhood, though not in the traditional sense.

I should be at home with my firstborn. Wires, hoses, and machines should be left at the hospital. Breathing should not be the main concern for this little wonder.

Yet tracing my finger across his forehead, I was in awe. This sweet boy was a miracle, and in this moment, I chose to revel in what God had given us. A life-giving, breathing miracle. Not of our choosing, but of God's.

I looked up from the comfort of the purple rocking chair and saw Ralph's face beaming down at me. Did he sense the preciousness of this moment too? Looking back at Samuel, his eyes were closed, enjoying the bliss of sleep.

Ralph tapped his watch. "We should leave soon."

I nodded. Needing time to devote to my husband, I know it was the right thing to place our son back in the crib, but how could I do this and not wake my sleeping angel?

Nodding to the hoses, Ralph took my cue to hold them while I stood. Taking baby steps, I lay my son down. The mattress accepted his weight. Startled by all the movement, my boy looked up at me and opened his mouth. If the trach would allow it, I knew the sound would be a piercing cry.

Trying not to pick him up again, I leaned over and cooed while stroking his arm.

His nurse Sandy arrived to silence the now-piercing alarm ringing above the crib. The effort to cry was requiring enough energy it was causing his oxygen levels to drop. Turning a dial to give my son more oxygen (the same one I'd touched earlier), the nurse turned to me.

"He must not want you to leave."

I nodded. "I guess not."

As his oxygen level stabilized, he stopped crying as I continued to run my finger over the rolling folds of skin on his arm. He was awake, but not fussy.

Ralph touched my shoulder. "He looks better now. Why don't we go home?"

Sandy nodded. "Yes, I agree. You two should go home and get some rest. I'll take good care of Samuel. I'll give him a bath, and he'll be ready to go to sleep afterwards."

I raised one eyebrow. Sandy continued, "Why don't you call me after you get home and I'll give you an update?"

Knowing I was not going to win this one, I agreed. We were both tired, and Samuel was comfortable. It made sense to go home. My heart didn't agree, but my body did.

Chapter 18

READY OR NOT, HERE WE GO

"Are you ready?"

Standing in the hallway, waiting to be buzzed into the PICU, I looked wearily at Ralph. Was I ready to spend the night in the PICU caring for Samuel?

"Yes, I guess so."

The huge white double doors swung open, allowing entrance in the sanctuary of the u-shaped unit. I headed toward Samuel's room. Approaching the nurses' station, Samuel's nurse greeted us.

"So are you two ready to watch Samuel tonight?"

I answered first. "Uh, yes, I think so."

Ralph nodded. "Sure."

She smiled a grin reminding me of a cat who captured a mouse. "You know, you both will be doing all of Samuel's care tonight. Of course, we are here if you need us, but the idea is for you to get comfortable with caring for Samuel at home. We aren't going to be at home with you, so you need to learn how to do this on your own."

Her speech brought me little comfort. I knew how to suction, I knew how to change his trach, and I knew how to make adjustments to the equipment, though Ralph was better at the last one than me. At least tonight we could touch the equipment without getting in trouble for it. If we're not able to handle ourselves tonight, I half wondered if they would release our almost six-month-old home to us.

Ralph moved closer to me. "We'll be fine."

Responding to Ralph, the nurse added, "Sorry, Dad, but we don't have a cot for you. Mom, you have the purple chair, and we put another chair in the room for you."

Entering the room, I saw my purple chair and two regular aluminum chairs with cushion padding on the back and bottom, reminding me of chairs in a waiting room. Looking at Ralph, he shrugged his shoulders. "I'll make it work."

Looking up at the monitors, none of the numbers were flashing red. Only green numbers greeted me. Good news. Leaning on the crib rail, Samuel was content to look at his mobile, which was switched off. I turned it on and watch the toy stuffed animals go around in circles. After the third went around, Samuel couldn't resist as he raised him arm to bat at the elephant as it swung by. I lifted my head, letting out a hearty laugh.

My goal was not to ask the nurses for help. I wanted to show them we could care for our little guy at home. Though, if he needed a saline treatment to loosen any phlegm in his chest, I'd need a nurse to get the saline for me.

The nurse provided us both throw blankets. After shutting off the overhead lights, I pulled the purple chair nearer the crib. Getting comfortable, I peeked every few moments to see if Samuel was still awake. I prayed for a smooth and easy night. One could always pray.

I awakened to the smell of eggs as Ralph placed a to-go container on the table next to my chair. I stretched, craning my neck to check Samuel. Sleeping beauty was still asleep. I didn't contemplate how I looked but allowed breakfast to call my name.

Thanking Ralph for the eggs and the surprise of a sweet roll he brought me from the cafeteria, I enjoyed breakfast. Now I needed a cup of tea, but before I could go to the break room, Dr. Lyon arrived. Did he ever sleep? Was there a cot somewhere I didn't know about?

"How did it go?"

I piped up, "Great. No alarms. Samuel slept soundly. We got about five hours' sleep."

Ralph snickered. "Speak for yourself. I got about two hours." We all looked at the chairs Ralph used and instantly knew his lack of sleep was attributed to his sleeping accommodations.

Dr. Lyon shook his head. "Sorry about that. We don't have cots available in the PICU."

As Ralph and Dr. Lyon chatted about ventilators, I tuned out their conversation. The ventilator intimidated me, but Ralph was intrigued by it.

I overheard Dr. Lyon tell Ralph he had a ventilator guru who was well versed in how to help children on vents. Once Samuel was released to go home, he suggested we come by the office and meet her. I was comforted to hear of Dr. Lyon's confidence in Samuel's release. The vent trials were going well, and the staff arranged for us to stay last night to test our skills, so I imagine they too were confident.

The doctor gave me a wave as he left Samuel's room. Ralph reminded me we were going to pick up a crib today. I nodded. This was another indicator our son would come home. I restrained my joy at the thought knowing he was not home until he was home.

"Ready to go?"

I touched Samuel's hand, marveling at its softness. I leaned over and placed a kiss on his forehead. Inhaling the smell of his scent, it reminded me of baby powder and lotion.

"Yes, let's go."

Ralph looked at the crib and shook his head. The store clerk stood next to him. They both pondered how to get the square box containing the crib to fit into the green Pontiac convertible.

The clerk pointed to the back. "Maybe you can put the convertible top down, and I can lay it in the backseat."

Looking at the darkening sky, I considered the wisdom of this idea.

Ralph shrugged his shoulders. "Let's try it."

After lowering the top, the clerk aided Ralph in lifting the heavy box into the backseat now exposed to the elements. It fit.

Ralph turned to me, flashing a broad smile. "Let's go."

I shook my head and returned his smile. I'd have to pray the skies wouldn't open up, drenching us all.

Pulling out of the parking lot, I had to pinch myself. We did it. One more step to bringing our miracle home. Even so, going through the motions of preparing for a homecoming didn't ease the sense that something could impede his departure from the hospital. For now, I'd rejoice in buying a crib like any other new parents.

On the way to meet Hector of DME Tampa Services, I quizzed Ralph how Samuel's fitting with the car seat went. Usually completed in the first three days of a baby's life, we were six months late.

"He seemed fine with it."

"I wish I could have been there."

"You had to work. Anyway, I was there. He did fine, really."

I tried to imagine our son swallowed up by the big brown car seat Anne bought. Where did they put all the tubing? Was it comfortable for him?

We arrived at DME Tampa Services to find out what equipment Samuel would need at home. Hector, a young man with an air of confidence, greeted us. After introductions, he covered everything we needed and somethings we weren't aware of. I listened intently but largely let Ralph field the meeting.

We left full of information and a peace knowing we had someone as knowledgeable and experienced as Hector.

Going to dinner allowed us to digest the meeting. Were we ready to bring our medically needy child home? Were we going to have all the equipment in place? What if we forgot something? Questions not answered but best left alone while I laid my trust in prayer. What else could I do?

Drawn back to the hospital, Ralph chatted with the respiratory therapist about the equipment while I cooed over Samuel. The nurse gave me an update, telling me he had a shot for RSV. The shot was to help prevent contracting the virus, which could be devastating for our son with such compromised lungs.

Relieved for protection from this potential roadblock in my son's health, I made a mental note to keep him away from any germs. I chuckled, because it seemed so improbable. Looking at my sweet son yawning and snuggling, I knew I would have to try.

After arriving home, Ralph read the Psalms to me. Hearing his voice read the comforting words calmed my soul. Blocking out all the competing thoughts in my mind, I snuggled deeper into my bed pillows.

I said a prayer. Sleep came quickly.

Stepping into Samuel's room, I found Ralph standing at the head the crib holding our son's trach in place with two fingers. My mouth gaped open as I saw a group of home health care nurses surrounding the crib.

"Hi, honey, you want to help with the trach change? We're showing these nurses how it's done."

Samuel's hospital nurse was grinning from ear to ear. Ralph had done the trach change three times before, but this time there was an audience.

I nodded. "Sure, be right there."

Washing my hands at the sink, I offered a quick prayer for everything to go well. Though it was routine to change Samuel's trach with a clean one, my stomach started to churn at the thought of something going wrong. Drying my hands, I held my breath and stepped opposite my husband.

Ralph nodded at the new trach lying next to Samuel's head. "I've got the new trach ready, and I've taken the ties off Samuel's current trach. You pull out the trach, and I'll put the new one in."

I nodded. *Oh, Lord, please help this go smoothly. Here goes.* I let out a breath and inhaled. Ralph moved his fingers, holding the trach, and I slid the plastic piece out of my son's neck. Once my hands were clear, Ralph slid the new trach in and pulled the obturator out.

Standing tall, Ralph grinned at his audience. I let out a long breath, happy the exchange was successful. We were not done yet, though, but the hard part was completed. Ralph leaned in and held the new trach as I threaded the trach tie through the right plastic hole and secured the Velcro onto the strap. Did the same for the left side, and we were done. Samuel didn't fuss at all. He lay there, no wiggling, no tears, no whining. A few nurses nodded to one another as they filed out of the room.

As his nurse cleaned up after the trach change, Ralph touched my elbow, leading me out the door. "We have a meeting to go to. Let's go."

I nodded. I remember this was the meeting to go over Samuel's discharge. Feeling the tension building in my shoulders, I rubbed the back of my neck. Would I be able to keep calm?

Arriving in the meeting room, there were a few familiar faces. Dr. Bravello, Hector from DME Tampa Services, along two nurses from Twin Lakes Nursing Services, the nursing agency. Again, allowing Ralph to take the lead, I listened.

Opening a binder, Nora, the hospital administrator, started reading from a checklist to be sure we had what we needed. Did we have nursing set up? The nurse from Twin Lakes Nursing Services interjected, "The staffing concerns for twenty-four-hour care are covered." Both nurses nodded. Ralph told me later Sunny Home Health Nursing didn't have enough nurses to meet Samuel's needs.

Did we have a car seat? Ralph confirmed we had a car seat and would do a second fitting after the meeting. As the checklist was read aloud, my shoulders released a little bit of its tension. Samuel was going to be released. This was happening. No one was trying to get him back to Skyfall. The sole purpose of the meeting was to have everything ready for his homecoming.

Then I heard something to make my head straighten up. The tone took me off guard at first. Then the full impact of the words hit me.

"You know," Nora lowered her voice, "releasing a child from the hospital doesn't work out so well all the time." She paused, and the room was silent. Tension flooded back into my shoulders as I braced my back against the chair.

"A child can be readmitted within six months."

Another nurse added, "Or even the same day. If anything concerns you while Samuel is at home, you can come back here. Don't feel bad. It happens all the time."

Like prickles on a porcupine, the hairs on my body rose. My son would not need to come back here. Not today, not for a long time. I didn't voice my thoughts because I feared I'd receive sympathetic looks, not understanding the circumstances. And though they might be right, I didn't fully comprehend Samuel's fragility, but I did understand God's strength. This was where I chose to rest.

I managed to smile and hold my tongue. As we left the meeting, one thought prevailed, *Let's watch what God can do.*

Entering Samuel's room, Ralph placed Samuel in the car seat. Within seconds, his face scrunched up and turned red. He opened his mouth and closed it. It was time to rescue my son by snatching him from the large beige car seat and rock him back and forth. I sat in the rocking chair and continued what I hope was a comforting movement. The redness went away, and Samuel's face relaxed. I thanked God for the change. After I laid him in the crib, his eyelids grew heavy. All the activity wore our little guy out. He was not the only one, but our list was too long to rest now. We had a homecoming to prepare for.

Ralph went home to receive the home ventilator and other emergency equipment we would need. Choosing to be by Samuel's side, I stayed at the hospital and searched the Internet for a glider to rock Samuel in. I had gotten used to the purple rocking chair at the hospital. I couldn't imagine not having a glider at home.

Finding a good deal on a glider for two hundred dollars, Ralph agreed to pick me up and go to the Super Target in New Tampa. We arrived before the store closed and managed to fit the box in our car.

Making it home, Ralph somehow found the energy to put it together. With the final bolt attached, I tried out the beige rocking chair, imagining Samuel in my arms. I wouldn't have to leave my house to visit my son somewhere else. I could get up in the middle of the night and tiptoe to his crib and watch him sleep. No more calls to find out how he was doing or using the NICU hall phone to be buzzed in.

As I pulled the comforter around me, I could hardly close my eyes thinking about my son's homecoming. My only fear was what would happen if something went wrong. I presented my concerns to God in a prayer and convinced myself to leave those cares in the hands of the one who holds Samuel. Now if I could only leave my cares there.

I awoke with one thought, *Samuel is coming home today.* My main goal was to bring our son home. I'd even scheduled the day off work so I could focus on the task at hand. Finally, my son would come home from the hospital.

Over a cup of hot tea, I closed my eyes as I listened to my husband's voice reading the Bible. The hot liquid radiated warmth, but the words stilled my soul, preparing me for the day ahead.

My husband closed the Bible and grabbed his coffee. We discussed the plan for the day. I'd go to the hospital while Ralph waited for Hector to set up the equipment at the rental house. The nurse from Twin Lakes Nursing Services would arrive at the house at noon. And Samuel would be released at noon.

Leaving the rental house, I couldn't help but grin from ear to ear. He was coming home. Joy filled my heart one moment and was mixed with apprehension of the unknown the next. Having my son home meant caring for our little guy twenty-four hours a day. Would I be a good special needs mom? Soon I'd find out.

Arriving at the hospital, I walked through the front doors. Would this be the last time I entered these doors? Could it be? Exhaling, I held to hope.

Today was the day.

As I entered the hospital room, light streamed in the window, giving off a warm glow. Slipping by my son's side, his hands batted at the mobile. My heart soared.

"Hi, Mom. Are you ready for today?"

Hearing the nurse's voice, I looked up and nodded. "Yes, very much."

"I'm sure you are. We are getting discharge papers together now. We just want to check Samuel's blood gas one more time before he goes. The techs will be here in a few minutes to do that. If everything goes well, he'll be released soon."

I exhaled. No sweeter words. Being told that the hospital only offered immediate care and was not an extended-care facility, I was thankful our son was able to go home. I could manage his care, touch the settings, and love my child up close and not part-time. I didn't even feel like a mother yet. A part-time mother, yes. I missed out on the first six months of raising a baby. Instead of dwelling on this, I looked forward to being a full-time mother.

The techs approached the metal frame crib and placed gauze, tape, and a pen needle on the mattress. I knew what was coming next. Try as I might, I could never get used to seeing my son's toe pricked for a blood sample. Stroking Samuel's arm, I leaned over and whispered in his ear, being sure not to watch the techs work.

Samuel didn't flinch, and the techs were done before I realized it. Had this gotten so routine for my wee one? With no tears. Would this be the last blood sample?

Almost time to go. Soon the ambulance would come. I was tempted to call Ralph. I'd wait a few more minutes.

Samuel's nurse approached me, holding a report in her hand. "We got the blood gas back. His pH is out of balance. The doctor thinks its best we keep Samuel here."

Several thoughts collided. What about the nurse waiting at the house? And Ralph waiting with Hector for our impending arrival. Was this temporary?

Seeing my crestfallen face, the nurse continued, "We are going to put Samuel on the LTV1000 hospital vent and do another blood gas in a few hours. If his gasses improve, we'll reschedule discharge for tomorrow."

Rubbing my forehead, I managed a "Thank you" to the nurse and sat down. I needed to call Ralph.

"Hi, honey. How's it going there?"

"Great. Hector and I have the LTV all set up and ready to go. The nurse is here. We were just waiting for you."

I closed my eyes. "Samuel is not coming home today. They are holding him because his blood gas came back with a high p H. They will try another blood gas in a few hours."

"They have got to make sure he's okay before they send him home, my love. Don't worry. I'll send the nurse and Hector home."

"Yes, hopefully he'll come home tomorrow."

After I hung up, I tried to make the best of it. Who said he'd come home on the first try? Should I have expected a delay? To cushion my heart, I decided to believe my son was released when he was finally in his crib at home. And pray.

I awoke wondering if Samuel would be released today. Reliving yesterday, I decided it was best not to get my hopes up. I had an early-morning meeting at work to keep me distracted.

Getting ready, I focused on the office meeting, but Samuel kept coming to mind. Ralph agreed to go to the hospital while I went to work. It was a plan; the rest was up to God.

Rushing to get to the meeting on time, I managed to arrive three minutes late. I slipped into an empty chair and was thankful my supervisor hadn't started yet. I chose to leave my phone on so I could be ready to take a call from the hospital. Everyone knew I was expecting Samuel to be released.

My manager started to speak. I tried to focus but found I couldn't concentrate. My mind was three miles away with my son. I shook my head and refocused. *Concentrate, Evelyn.* Taking a deep breath, I exhaled and listened. As each agenda was covered, I checked them off.

After the last topic was covered and we were dismissed, I scurried to my desk. My work laptop read 9:00a.m. How much longer should I wait to hear? Should I call and get an update? I resisted the urge and focused on work instead.

I stayed distracted as each task came in. Work was in all-in proposition, so I was not surprised I could keep from obsessing about Samuel's release.

Bing, I heard my phone, alerting me to an incoming message. Placing my work phone on hold, I access my messages on my cell phone. It was Ralph telling me Samuel's discharge was a go. I closed my eyes and exhaled. Yes, it was finally happening.

I logged out of my phone and informed my supervisor I was leaving for the day. She wished me good luck, and I was out the door in minutes.

When I arrived in Samuel's room at the hospital, people were everywhere. Ralph greeted me grinning. Samuel was snug in his car seat and not crying. I pointed to my son and raised my eyebrows. Ralph explained he put a towel in the car seat to support his back like when he was in the crib. That was the secret to keeping him happy in the car seat.

As word got out in the PICU of Samuel's departure, nurses from the ward came to hug me good-bye and shake Ralph's hand. Words were offered, "We hope we don't see you again, at least not here" or "Good luck." But one hospital administrator cornered me, giving me his speech.

Perhaps he had given this speech before. As he continued his tirade, I silently repeated "He'll surprise you" and willed myself to keep calm.

"You know, your son will be back here. He will catch a cold, and we will need to treat him." Taking my silence for acceptance, he continued, "You know, the germs in the hospital are different from the germs in your home."

Was he telling me this because he thought Samuel wouldn't handle the transition?

Out of the corner of my eye, I saw an EMS worker pull a wagon with Samuel's things out of the room. I assumed he was going to the ambulance. Refocusing on the administrator, he droned on.

"So just know it's completely normal for a discharged patient to be readmitted after they leave. We're here when you need us."

Offering a pursed smile, he excused himself, leaving me relieved of his absence. If he could only read my thoughts, he'd be appalled. No way was my son returning. My son had beaten every odd thrown at him. Why would I think he'd return, fulfilling this man-made prophesy? Why I believed my son wouldn't return was an inner gift from God.

One of the two EMTs returned to the room, placing Samuel on the stretcher. He used one hand on the car seat to keep it in place. The second EMT arrived. With a nod, he asked, "Ready to go?"

As the nurses nodded in the affirmative, I sought out Ralph's face. He too nodded, adding a goofy grin. Should I pinch myself? We were really leaving this place. Home was where my son should be. For so long it had been out of reach. And even yesterday, it was snatched away, but not today.

With a final hug to Samuel's nurse Kelly, I followed the stretcher out of the room. I briefly looked back at the stark-white walls of the room with now-silent equipment and black monitor screens. Without Samuel, it looked devoid of life, a vast wilderness to which I pray he would never return. Though this room had been the only home Samuel had known, it was time to introduce him to a real home, where Mommy and Daddy would care for him, even in the wee hours of the morning.

Now in go mode, I followed the EMTs to the ambulance. Loading Samuel up into the back of the ambulance, I slipped next to my son as

Ralph followed in my black Honda. Turning onto the main highway, an alarm blared as my son's oxygen level drops. Reacting to the sound, the EMT disconnected Samuel's tubing attached to the ventilator and used the blue Ambu bag to manually give Samuel oxygen.

My heart caught in my throat. I went into prayer mode while touching Samuel's hand, something to connect us together while I relied on God to answer a mother's prayer. The thought of returning to the hospital never crossed my mind. I was too busy praying.

Samuel's numbers went up slowly. I exhaled and whispered a quiet "Thank you" to God when the EMT placed Samuel back on the ventilator.

What was my son thinking as he looked around the ambulance? Did he remember his last ambulance ride brought him to Skyfall Pediatric Center? I shuddered at the thought.

Leaning close to Samuel, I spoke by his ear, "Samuel, you're going home. Wait until you see your new room. And Daddy is waiting for us."

My words, though meant to comfort Samuel, gave me something to do, a way to help make my son know I was here. I was familiar, and this bouncing boat ride of an ambulance was temporary, bringing our son to a warm and loving place far from hospitals and institutional environments.

Another alarm broke my reverie, and my prayers were once again activated. The EMT followed the same protocol. In minutes, the numbers were green, and the ventilator was reattached. My heart broke as I saw a tear slip from my son's eyes. *Oh, Lord, how much longer before we're home?*

Coming to a major stoplight, we waited for the light to turn green. I knew this was a normal transport home and didn't warrant the sirens to be activated, but I wished they were on.

I breathed a sigh of relief as traffic flowed north. Thinking the rest of the trip should be event free, I relaxed against the bulkhead of the ambulance and closed my eyes. I jumped when I heard the alarms sound off. Tears were now streaming from Samuel's eyes as his mouth opened in a silent cry.

The EMT performed his usual routine in an effort to help my son breathe. I held back my own tears wanting to be brave for Samuel and praying we arrived soon. The numbers once again rose, and my son's face relaxed as tears flowed to a trickle.

The EMT driving the ambulance shouted, "We're here!"

Oh, thank God.

The EMT's leaped into action. One continued to Ambu Samuel while the other pulled out the stretcher, pushing it up the drive to the open door of our rental home.

Hector, a training aide; Kathy, the nurse; and Ralph were waiting to accept our precious package. Everyone sprang into action. The EMTs transferred him to the awaiting crib Ralph so lovingly put together. Hector turned on the ventilator as the EMT disconnected the Ambu bag, and Kathy was scurrying about to care for her new charge.

As a ray of sunshine streamed into the living room, Samuel blinked at his new surroundings. His lips curled into a grin. I broke out laughing at the scene before me. My whole body shook with joy. Ralph grabbed his camera in an effort to capture the scene forever, burning this day in our memory.

Pushing aside all thoughts of returning to the hospital, my joy broke out into a silent prayer of thanks for my miracle son to be in our home. The day I'd wonder would ever come had arrived. Samuel was now in our living room. Today, we celebrated.

Tomorrow, we would work to keep our son home.

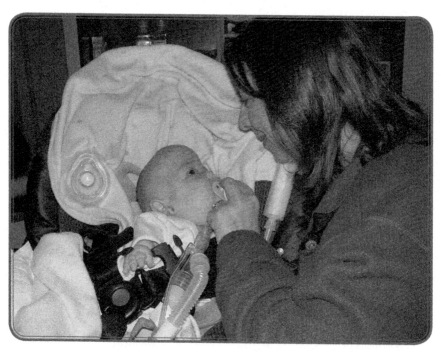

Miracle In My Living Room

E p i l o g u e

On August 2, 2006, another miracle happened. My son turned one years old. Exceeding all expectations from the medical community, we celebrated with great joy and lots of balloons. And though we heard the staff were betting my son would return to the hospital, he eviscerated those expectations.

We were given another gift in the form of a phone call. The doctor who predicted Samuel's demise called. Speaking to Ralph, he said, "All children are different." I stored this treasure in my heart as his apology to us. Indeed, all children are different. My son defied all the odds, and a miracle happened. They do happen. My son is proof.

After his release from the hospital, Samuel's environment was contained to being at home or visiting a long list of doctors.

Then when Samuel turned three years old, he was nominated to receive a wish. Maria Mendevill, a Make-A-Wish volunteer, and Joe Pearl, the father of a wish child, came to our home to assess what wish would be granted. They asked many questions about Samuel's interests. I shared Samuel enjoys balloons and the huge fish mural painted on the wall in his bedroom.

A few weeks later, Maria and Joe came to our church fellowship hall to announce Samuel's wish. They brought lots of balloons and an envelope revealing we were going to Sea World.

Before we knew it, the time came for us to go on our seven-day adventure. On a cold day in January, a limo pulled in front of our home to transport us to Orlando, such a big limo for a little guy with dwarfism. We filled half of the huge limo with our luggage and

Samuel's medical equipment, which included his ventilator, suction equipment, oxygen tanks, Ambu bag, and backup batteries.

We were driven to Give Kids The World Village in Orlando, a resort for wish families staffed by loving volunteers. We were given our own villa as well as tickets to not only Sea World but to all the other theme parks as well. What a surprise.

Each day, my husband and I would venture out with Samuel several times. At home, it was overwhelming to go out once a week to visit Samuel's doctors, and now we were leaving three times a day. We learned very quickly we needed a checklist to be sure we didn't leave any of Samuel's life-saving equipment in the villa.

We visited Sea World, Disney World, the Rainforest Café, and many other attractions, but a couple of moments stand out.

While at Disney, I needed to change Samuel. My husband waited outside while I walked down a long walkway to find the ladies' room. Once there, I laid Samuel down and then reached under the stroller for a diaper. I search everywhere and didn't find a diaper. I looked at the mom next to me changing her daughter. In my desperation, I asked her for a diaper. She graciously offered me one. Later I laughed. We had all of Samuel's medical equipment but forgot the one thing you should never leave the home without: a diaper.

Another time, we were deep in Disney World as I was pushing Samuel's stroller near a water pond. I stopped, listened to the hum of Samuel's ventilator, and looked out over the water. A thought of panic overtook me. Were we crazy doing this? What if something happened? How was an ambulance going to find to us here? I turned to look at Samuel and found him sleeping. Everything was fine. I needed to learn to relax and enjoy the gift of our son's life.

It was during this wish I discovered that being pushed out of my comfort zone was not only good for me but for Samuel as well, who was discovering a whole new world he never knew existed. He saw dolphins close up, had pictures taken with Mickey Mouse and Goofy, and enjoyed his first merry-go-round ride.

Yes, it was a vacation, but it was more than that for us. It was a training ground, teaching us how to live a more normal life with a medically needy child.

A few weeks after we came home, my husband again asked me, "Can we take him to the park now?" My first impulse was to say no, but then I remembered our trip to Disney. "Yes, we can go."

And go we did. To the park, to Lowry Park Zoo, and to the Florida Marine Aquarium.

My son is now eleven years old. He is still a little guy at twenty-five pounds, twenty-five inches, but he has a big personality with a smile that melts hearts. We have been on several trips now. From taking Samuel to Niagara Falls and Washington, DC, to traveling to Prince Edward Island in Canada.

These are the miracles that happened in our living room and in the world beyond it.

Samuel's Impact

Pastor Steve Hogan

Ralph and Evelyn have been a wonderful example and inspiration to our church. We have seen them trusting the Lord for the impossible. We have seen their love for Samuel. We have seen their day after day, month after month, year after year faithfulness and perseverance, serving and caring for their little God given child. And when I say faithful, I mean 24-7, day after day, night after night. Dad and Mom were always with Samuel, feeding him, picking him up, dressing him, and taking him for walks; and then there were tubes, monitors, and lots of diapers and runny noses.

What a blessing it has been for my life, and for our church, to have this special family, Ralph, Evelyn and Samuel, be part of our church family. There is no doubt this family has been an expression of God's kindness and for this we are very thankful.

Little Samuel brings great joy to our church family. Sunday after Sunday we see him with his contagious little smile, scooting here and there, nimbly going after his cheerios, navigating on his iPad, and he even gives us high fives. All children are a blessing, but Samuel, he is a special blessing, a child our church has come to truly love and enjoy. That he has been with us now for over 11 years is absolutely amazing and a testimony to the work of our heavenly Father and a testimony to the work of Samuel's faithful and loving parents, Ralph and Evelyn.

Michele Jewell, Mother of Luke, Survivor to Age Twenty

My life thinking has been impacted by Samuel Mann and his parents, Ralph and Evelyn Mann, because of a similar situation our sons shared. Samuel is a little boy diagnosed with Thanatophoric Dysplasia (TD), the same diagnosis our son Luke was given at birth in 1987. Even though we were told our son would not live but only a few hours, a few days at best, he overcame and lived for 20 years. Likewise, Samuel is well on his way with a similar joyous attitude towards being the best he can be.

Our son, along with another boy named Thomas, another girl named Siri, and another boy named Jan (John) and some others we have read about and heard about seem to have forged the trail, teaching us so much about living life on a respirator. Given a chance, these children overcame hurdles that were thought impossible. Samuel has gone one step further and weaned off the respirator. What a victory!

This is hardly believable given the prognosis. It is one thing we had hoped Luke would be able to do. Now that it has been accomplished I have a hope that what we are learning will be passed along to help the next one.

Our family is happy to hear about and see Samuel as he grows up and also another boy Charlie whose diagnosis is also TD. Charlie is maneuvering his own wheelchair with a joy stick! All of these children with TD, and there are more, have greatly inspired me along with the invested lives of their parents, siblings and caregivers. Our children are a gift from God. It is good to see Samuel's life handed the 'torch', to run on with this diagnosis and make the whole Thanatophoric Dysplasia 'family' proud. I am blessed to see these other families be as blessed as we were. Raising a child with special needs is hard work, a labor of love and so worth it.

I am amazed when I consider how God crossed our paths so our families could meet each other back in 2009. When our youngest son, Joey, needed to write a paper at school he was perusing the internet in hopes of finding the published article of our son Luke in the American Journal of Medical Genetics. Instead he found Evelyn's blog. The attached picture in the description looked like Luke. Clicking on the link, thinking someone had put a picture of Luke on the internet; imagine our happy surprise to read instead about Samuel. It was a special day when we were finally able to meet Samuel and his parents in person. These children who have been diagnosed with this extremely rare form of what is considered a lethal dwarfism, have linked our families together forever.

Samuel Mann, we are so very glad to know you! Luke James Jewell, we greatly miss you, RIP. 03/24/1987-10/27/2007.

~Michele Jewell, wife of Jim Jewell, mother of Jenifer (Mikael), Laura (Scott), Luke, Joseph and grandmother of Anneli, Emmiline, and Sylvia.

Carol Russo, Mother of Thomas, Survivor to Twenty-Six Years Old

Seeing Samuel makes my day. He makes me smile. I see so much of my angel Thomas in him. And that warms my heart. My amazing miracle Thomas was always happy and smiling. He touched people's lives all over the world like Samuel. Thomas was vent and oxygen dependent all his life until he passed away at age 26, four years ago. Always in my heart.

Jacquelynn Sierra, Mother of Devan, Survivor to Age Four

Evelyn is such a wonderful woman, and I can honestly say that watching her son, Samuel grow up has been a blessing for me. I miss my Devan every day, but watching Samuel and seeing his pictures and videos, well I like to imagine a little piece of my Devan lives on through Samuel. Thank you, Evelyn, for sharing and giving a voice for all of the mothers who have had to go through something similar. I pray God always watches over you and your beautiful family.

Lana Magee, Mother of Collin

I remember the comforting feeling that came over me from reaching out to Evelyn when I had Collin. Even before Collin was born, Samuel gave me hope. I would go to Evelyn's website all the time and loved seeing pictures and updates. He made me feel like whatever Collin's outcome, life could still be beautiful. I remember the feeling I got when I saw Evelyn responded to my email. All of a sudden, I wasn't alone in this as a mother to a TD baby. I'm forever thankful for Samuel and for Evelyn sharing his story. It's pretty amazing what she does for others.

Dominika Wilkins, Mom of TD Baby-to Be Willow

When I was first informed of TD by the specialist, she told me it is lethal in all cases. She explained it's not genetic because nobody has lived long enough to pass the gene. (It is a random genetic mutation.) She told me this is a death sentence and essentially convinced me not to have hope. So, that's what happened. I lost all hope, and I mean there was not a single speck of hope in my soul. But once I discovered you and Samuel, I could feel my soul lighting up a little. To know that the Greek meaning of Thanatophoric is death bearing, yet there are people who are alive and striving with this very condition is just amazing. You can't help but to gain hope at that point.

I was in a meeting with the specialist, head nurse and case management director of the hospital and all three kept telling me not to have hope. "Nobody survives this," they all said. Until I told them about Samuel and the others you have informed me of. The room fell silent at that point. I looked at the specialist and said "Samuel is eleven years old and there are some who are older than him." I thought her jaw was going to hit the floor. She had nothing to say but, "Wow, I had no idea." I didn't hear her or anyone else in the room try to convince me I shouldn't have hope again.

I don't think you or anyone could fully understand the impact you have had on my outlook.

After discovering that my unborn son would not be expected to live more than a few hours if at all I lost all hope and those who know me know that hope is something I can find in any situation however in this case I felt like I was digging and digging to no prevail until the day I discovered Samuel's story. It was like a light sparked inside my soul and I could smile again, every time I see a picture or video of Samuel and his beautiful smile I swear my heart skips a beat and I feel like everything is going to be okay no matter the outcome. Thank you Samuel for being the strong fighter that you are, I couldn't face my battle without your sweet smile.

Kayla Eastman, Soon-to-Be Mother of Josiah

Hearing your sons story has impacted me in more ways than one. I hope and pray my sweet Josiah turns out to be the next Samuel. Because of you and your son, I'm not giving up. I believe Josiah isn't either.

Much love.
Kayla, Josiah, Leo and Chris.

Cindy Placide, Mother of Isabelle, Survivor to Two Months

When my daughter was first diagnosed with Thanatophoric Dysplasia at birth, I felt hopeless. I had never heard of TD before. I was pulled in different directions. However, I first heard of Samuel through the nurses at the hospital, my first thought was there is hope for her. Your visit from Florida to Georgia was encouraging. Meeting your family and hearing Samuel's story and your journey with him growing up with TD, I was inspired.

Both you and your husband had a warm gentle spirit and I fell in love with Samuel. To see your son interact with you, his joy, happy disposition and love for life, I grew wings. I felt empowered, determined, found renewed confidence to fight for a better standard of living for my Izzie and on fire to get her help she needed from a respirator to a tracheotomy and home with us. Being a single mother already with a son with Autism I knew it was going to be a tough road ahead with them both but I was ready give her the best life possible; and knew that if your special needs child could be this happy, then I could provide the same atmosphere for my daughter Isabelle.

Sadly, she passed away a week later but though grieving I am working to do things in her memory. I'm presently in process of starting a nonprofit organization to help grieving and struggling moms with special needs kids and also writing a book of Poems among other things.

It gives me great joy to watching Samuel progress the past year and seeing Evelyn's continued fight to bring the message and recognition of TD and families affected by it through her blog and her book.

Thank you dear friend.

Samantha Holloway, Mother of Na'Vita, Survivor to Four and a Half Days

I wish that I would have known everything I know now. The day I found out my daughter had TD wasn't the hardest, the day she died wasn't the hardest. Every single day is the hardest knowing she isn't here. To know that Samuel is here makes me have hope. He makes my heart know that there's hope for others. A (tracheostomy) tube can and did save him.

The doctor that delivered my daughter came into my room AFTER I was totally elated from hearing her cry and being born alive and was still breathing on her own to ask me, "Why didn't I abort her, it's not natural, like what made you go through with everything?" I responded, "She's alive right!" Na'Vita lived four and a half more days.

If I would have done what Samuel had done she "may" still be with us, but that's the difference in every case of TD, you never know what kind of treatment they need. Many choose to use nothing, and let their baby live as long as they can be breathing completely alone. Others get a CPAP and they're good with a little help. Others may need a tracheostomy like Samuel. I say go for it, look at him. He smiles and giggles. He uses a tablet. He's a miracle.

I think about Samuel every moment I think of my daughter Na'Vita. Samuel is my light at the end of the tunnel. At times, I pray to God that I could do it all over again and do everything Evelyn did for Samuel for my daughter. I was scared and uneducated on this condition. I did research but there's not much out there.

Thanks to Samuel, I was given hope during my pregnancy. Na'Vita is watching over him as an angel. I have watched him grow up on social media and am amazed at every milestone he has accomplished. I am most positive it is because he has the strongest set of parents in this world. I know Samuel is just as proud of his parents as I am of him.

God bless you Samuel, may you continue to grow and beat the odds for all TD babies.

Angel Chartier, Mother of Michael Angelo, Survivor to Four Months

I am the mother of an Angel baby named Michael Angelo whom was born with Thanatophoric Dysplasia. My son's life ending after two months while in the NIU. During the time I was pregnant, I researched his condition only to learn his it was fatal. I felt nothing but hopelessness. Weeks after Michael was born, I found a You Tube video on a baby with TD swimming, smiling and living. I couldn't believe what I was seeing. I had to contact the mother to find out everything I could about the amazing baby. The babies name was Christian. After talking to the mother, she put me in contact with several other mothers with living children. I was astounded by these mothers and their children.

That night, I spoke over the phone with Evelyn. She shared information I would have never know about TD. She also sent me pictures and videos of Samuel. I get emotional. She told me she knew a nurse in my home town who had a TD child which lived to nearly five years. Turned out he was born in the same hospital nearly ten years earlier. Finally, for the first time I had hope. Evelyn and I spoke on nearly a daily basis. She often asked me, "How are you doing today? How is Michael doing? Are you encouraged?"

Learning of Samuel and the other living TD children changed our world. We were very discouraged by the doctors and bad information we were given. Knowing Samuel and other TD children were defying the odds gave us hope and encouragement allowing us to enjoy the time we had with our son. Through the work of Evelyn and Samuel spreading his love and encouragement to other mothers is an amazing blessing to all TD babies and parents.

Hope's Mum, Mother of Hope, Survivor to One hour and Thirty-Six minutes, Ireland

Too often the medical profession gives up on children that they define as having "a fetal abnormality" or as "incompatible with life." Many parents do not receive the information on survival and are often pushed towards abortion.

Parents receiving a diagnosis of Thanatophoric Dysplasia need to receive the most update information and made aware that although rare there are survivors in our world. One of these survivors is Samuel.

Samuel is 11 and enriches the life of all he touches. He reminds us, whatever small percentage of survival you have been given, there is Hope in the midst of despair . . .

Samuel is thriving on his own terms and defies those who fail to acknowledge his existence. He fills his parent's life with love, laughter, tears and worry just like every other child.

It is for these reasons we need to inform, update, and educate our friends, our family and the medical profession. Samuel reminds us that every life is precious and is not defined by a diagnosis. Not everything you read about TD is up to date/correct or black and white. There is life after a diagnosis of TD.

I pray that Samuel's story is a read around the world by the medical professionals dealing with babies/children with TD. May they start to acknowledge survival and inform parents there is hope for their baby. This will be the first step in changing the hearts and minds of those we entrust with the management/care of our pregnancy.

Hope's Mummy

Erin Davison, Mother of Charlie, Age Six

The Boys

Samuel Mann and his family are an inspiration for Thanataphoric dysplasia families. His life gives hope to those who are told their unborn baby will have TD. Through email and Facebook, we were touched by Samuel. When our son, Charlie, was diagnosed with TD, we researched and found the Mann family. We wanted to know what the doctors did not or could not tell us. We wanted hope and a chance to give our son a life. Samuel gave us hope and God gave our son life. We thank the Mann family for sharing Samuel's story with our family. As our sons grow in years, we hope their lives inspire and gives hope to others.

Thank you.
Love in Christ Jesus,
Erin and Mark Davison

Sareta-Beth Mc Rann, Mother of Christian, Survivor to Three and a Half Years

I was almost five months pregnant when I found out I was pregnant with Christian. At six months,

I found out he was going to be born with dwarfism. On January 25th, 2011, I was told Christian had thanatophoric dysplasia type 1 and I would have to abort. At this point, I just couldn't handle doctors. I was not going to abort my baby.

I Googled and researched what Thanatophoric Dysplasia (is). I found Evelyn and Samuel. I found Michelle, Laura and Luke. I found hope in my decision. Evelyn guided us to others and helped us in so many ways on our journey. We got 3 1/2 amazing years. I would do it all over again if I had the chance. I feel like I still have Christian. Like he is still alive in these children with TD. Samuel and Charlie are amazing. Samuel is change. Hoping with his progress he will keep giving hope.

Camilla Ferreira, Mother of David, Brazil

Knowing the history of the great warrior Samuel boosted my faith, because God gave me David with TD. When David was born, the doctors spoke that he would not pass from 1 week of life. With the passage of time, I got to know the history of the Samuel. All feelings of fear and doubt was gone and in place came to faith, belief and hope. When I see pictures and videos of Samuel, *me emociono*. Because I am sure that the God we serve and truly the God of the impossible, and that even if we have diversities we will win.

Darlene E. Kreke-Dahms, Mother of Owen, Survivor to Five Hours and Twenty-Three Minutes

I was grieving the loss of my little Owen when I came across a support group for families who have or had a

TD baby. It took me a few years or so to seek out other families who have gone through the same heartbreak. From what I understood there weren't many. I just wanted someone who knew what I had been through with that type of diagnosis to share my Owen with and just how special and unique he really was, is.

All I knew was that babies who are have TD die either before or shortly after. My little Owen lived for only 5 hrs & 23 min. We were blessed to have that time with him and see him open his eyes. We were told it was a miracle in and of itself.

When I came across Evelyn and Samuel, I couldn't believe what I was seeing. I was in awe of this beautiful little boy. I saw my Owen in him, in what could have been. He has helped me get through some of my grief I was holding back.

I see Samuel and I see a little boy who is strong willed and has a lot of fight in him. He is living proof that we still don't know all there is to know about TD. The medical community is still advancing in the unknown. All life is precious and should have every opportunity to survive. I believe that Samuel is a miracle for all to see. Even though TD, means death (bringing), he lived to prove differently even if it isn't easy.

He always has such a beautiful smile on his face, showing the world he will not be beaten easily. Samuel has so much life, spunkiness, love, and so much more to keep showing us how important it is to find out more. He just amazes me everyday I see his sweet face. He's such a little fighter!

Sydnie Keegan, Samuel's Facebook Fan

If there is any family who is truly a testament of God's love and a family's faith . . . the Mann family is living proof. I adore Mr. Samuel and the blogs of sharing their families' everyday life from Ms. Evelyn are absolutely inspirational.

The world needs to know about your families' everyday life with Samuel. And I, for one, have been truly blessed and honored that you've shared your journey of love, fears, Samuel's accomplishments and although few, the hard days.

You raising Samuel has been way more blessings and happiness. For that, I applaud your families' faith in trusting God's gift to the right family. But God already knew who He was going to be blessedly by giving you Samuel.

Carrie Gotfried Guise, Samuel's Therapist

He has grown so much. He taught me to never give up with a child as you never know what they are capable of doing. I really get excited when he makes progress no matter how small it might be. Samuel makes me realize how special a life can be.

About the Author

velyn Mann is a blogger, speaker, special needs child advocate, and author of her debut memoir, *Miracle In My Living Room*.

Evelyn Mann is a member of Word Weavers and has been published in many different mediums. She has been a keynote speaker for Make-A-Wish and her blog has over 1.3 million hits. She receives inquiries from around the world asking about her son's miraculous survival.

Raised on a 41-foot sailboat, Evelyn has a lifelong fondness for being near the water, making her home in Florida a perfect fit. She enjoys reading and blogging usually with a hot cup of tea.

Her loves are God, her husband, and her miracle son.

To contact Evelyn, please use the contact form at
www.miraclemann.com

You can also follow Samuel's journey on Facebook at
www.facebook.com/amiraclemann

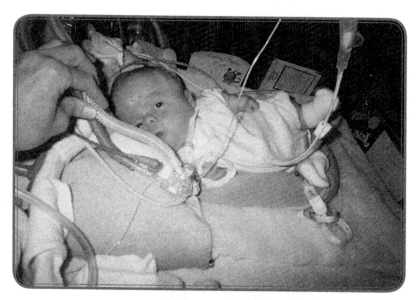

2 weeks old. Pre-tracheostomy.

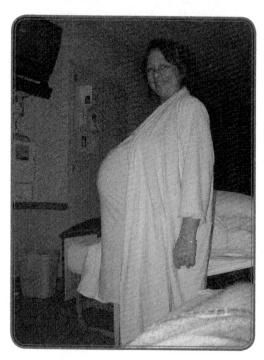

Ready to go! 35 weeks pregnant.

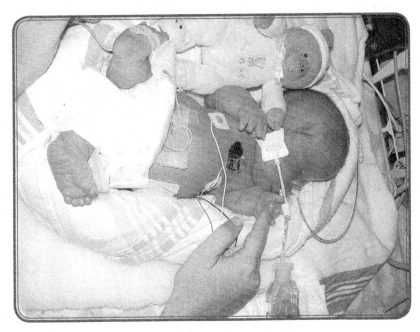
Tiny Mann- fierce determination.

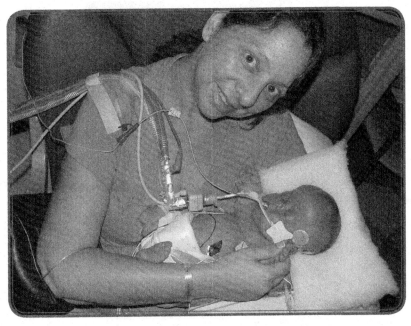
Mommy love - little miracle.

Peace in the midst of chaos.

Mike Alstott signed mini-helmet.

Christmas Joy - with no ventilator.

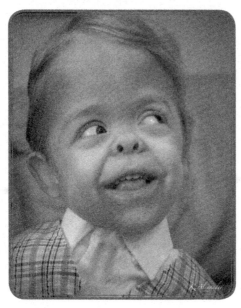

Do I look like a big boy, Mommy?

Joy in the journey.

CPSIA information can be obtained
at www.ICGtesting.com
Printed in the USA
LVOW13s1347200817

545694LV00011B/542/P